Bold
&
Blessed

Bold & Blessed

How to Stay True to Yourself and
Stand Out from the Crowd

TRINITEE STOKES

WITH CRYSTAL BOWMAN AND TERI MCKINLEY

ZONDERVAN

Bold and Blessed
Copyright © 2019 by Trinitee Stokes

Requests for information should be addressed to:
Zonderkidz, 3900 *Sparks Dr. SE, Grand Rapids, Michigan 49546*

Library of Congress Cataloging-in-Publication Data

Names: Stokes, Trinitee, author.
Title: Bold and blessed : how to stay true to yourself and stand out from
    the crowd / Trinitee Stokes, with Crystal Bowman and Teri McKinley.
Description: Grand Rapids : Zonderkidz, 2018. | Includes bibliographical
    references and index. |
Identifiers: LCCN 2018037386 (print) | LCCN 2018043873 (ebook) |
    ISBN 9780310766476 | ISBN 9780310766421 (softcover : alk. paper) |
    ISBN 9780310768401 (audio download : alk. paper)
Subjects: LCSH: Girls—Conduct of life--Juvenile literature. | Girls—
    Religious life—Juvenile literature. | Self-esteem in children—Juvenile
    literature. | Self-esteem—Religious aspects—Christianity—Juvenile
    literature.
Classification: LCC BV4551.3 (ebook) | LCC BV4551.3 .S76 2018 (print) |
    DDC 248.8/2—dc23

Scripture quotations are taken from the Holy Bible, New International
Version®, NIV®. Copyright © 1973, 1978, 1984, 2011 by Biblica, Inc.®
Used by permission of Zondervan. All rights reserved worldwide. www
.Zondervan.com. The "NIV" and "New International Version" are
trademarks registered in the United States Patent and Trademark Office
by Biblica, Inc.®

Any Internet addresses (websites, blogs, etc.) and telephone numbers in this
book are offered as a resource. They are not intended in any way to be or
imply an endorsement by Zondervan, nor does Zondervan vouch for the
content of these sites and numbers for the life of this book.

Published in association with Fox Rothschild LLP, California/New York/Wash-
ington DC/Nevada/Florida/Pennsylvania/Colorado/New Jersey/Connecticut/
Delaware/Texas.

Interior design: Denise Froehlich

Printed in the United States of America

---

18 19 20 21 22 23 /LSC/ 10 9 8 7 6 5 4 3 2 1

To my mom and dad—thank you for all the hard work you invest in me and for continually pouring into my dreams. You always put me first and none of this would be possible without you. I love you beyond words!

—TRINITEE

Contents

Foreword

BY ANGELA BASSETT

Have you ever seen a shooting star? The amazing brilliance of its light immediately captures your attention as you watch the spectacular "show in the sky." Meeting Trinitee Stokes is just like seeing this shooting star. Her intriguing and captivating personality immediately fills the room like a fireball of light as she radiates confidence, joy, and wisdom well beyond her 12 years.

Trinitee's book, *Bold and Blessed: How to Stay True to Yourself and Stand Out from the Crowd,* is her personal gift of shining light to young girls everywhere. Her book gives each girl one of the greatest gifts possible: the right to dream! In reading Trinitee's book, each girl is going to be guided toward humble self-confidence, encouraged to discover who she is as a spiritual being, and reminded she is FEARFULLY AND WONDERFULLY MADE!

If you are a parent, I urge you to let Trinitee speak to your daughter as this young soul's words of simple wisdom and faith teach positivity, obedience, and dedication. As each page motivates your daughter to stand UP and stand OUT, as each page lights a fire in her belly and tells her to "bring your best YOU," as each page draws her to strive for her limitless potential; I know you will join me in celebrating the endless wonders she will achieve.

Introduction

Hey, Friends!

I am super excited that you picked up this book because I wrote it just for you! You might know me from my role on a Disney TV show, or maybe you've seen me in some commercials. I'm also a singer and fashion designer. You are probably wondering what it's like to live in Hollywood and work as an actress while still being a kid. That's why I wanted to write this book! In each chapter, I'll take you behind the scenes to give you a peek into my life on and off the screen. I'll share some fun tips on fashion and hair, and include some trivia, girl advice, or a short activity just for you. I've also asked some of my favorite people—my fans and supporters—to send in questions for this book. Each chapter includes a Q & A with real questions from people like you who helped me get where I am today.

Even though my life may seem glamorous on the outside, I'm just a regular girl trying to figure things out. I care about my family and friends. I have hobbies and interests and schoolwork, and sometimes I have tough stuff to deal with—just like you. I want to talk about how all those pieces of our lives—the good and the bad—make us who we are.

Because here's the thing—my acting and singing career didn't just happen. I had dreams and goals that God put on my heart, and I worked very hard to achieve them. I still work hard every day to keep fulfilling my destiny. I bet you have some dreams and goals too! Throughout this book, I'll be sharing some ways that you can work toward seeing *your* dreams come true.

This book isn't just about me—it's also about you. You can learn how to be strong and confident. You can learn how to be your own person and not be influenced by people who try to discourage your dreams. You can do whatever you set your mind to—if you are willing to work at it and pray through it. You don't have to wait until you're all grown up to be somebody special or do important things. You are special right now, and you have gifts and talents that you can use!

You, my friend, are wonderfully made by God!

You are so unique that there is no one in the world exactly like you. Whether you are eight or twelve or nineteen, I want to encourage you to be all that God has created you to be. I hope that as you read this book, you will learn how to be *BOLD* so you can be *BLESSED!*

Smooches, Trinitee

CHAPTER 1

Hello World! It's Me, Trinitee

BEHIND THE SCENES

Some of you know me as Judy, the little sister in the Cooper family from the Disney show *K.C. Undercover*. Disguised as Judy Cooper, I play the part of a sophisticated humanoid robot who helps the family solve undercover missions. That's my character on screen. But what I really want to tell you about is who I am in real life.

My name is Trinitee Stokes and I was born in Jackson, Mississippi. My name was supposed to be Tanae. My parents were so set on using that name that it's in all the pictures from my mom's baby shower. But during delivery, the doctor discovered that the umbilical cord was wrapped around my neck three times. I think it's because I was always dancing around in the womb when my mom went in for sonograms! As my mom was lying on the delivery table and learned about the cord, she thought of the Trinity—the name for God being three in one—Father, Son, and Holy Spirit. So, she changed my name to Trinitee, with a different spelling, to remind us that God had his hand on my life. I could have died, but I didn't. My life began with a God experience, and Trinitee became my name. When I became an actress, I chose The Trinitee for my stage name so that whenever someone calls my name, they can be reminded of the biblical Trinity. Sometimes people ask me about my name and it gives me a chance to talk about Jesus.

I think I have always wanted to be an actress. When I was only two years old, I was watching a funny episode of *That's So Raven*, and it made me laugh so hard. I told my mom, "I want to be on TV, so I can make people laugh too."

When I was three years old, my mom wrote her first theater play with a few of her church friends. The name of the play was "What Kind of Christmas

Is This?" She created the role of a little girl named Tiana just for me. Tiana was the youngest of four children and was wise beyond her years. It was the perfect part for me! I loved playing Tiana on stage, and everyone said I stole the show.

Two years later, my parents found an agent for me in Jackson, and my professional acting career began. My first real acting job was a Maxwell House coffee commercial that was filmed in New Orleans. Soon after that, my agent brought in some agents from Los Angeles and New York so they could meet child actors from the area. Some of the children got offers from an agent, but all of the agents wanted me to sign with them because they said I had the "it" factor. I didn't really know what that meant at the time, but I was beyond excited that I had a shot at an acting career. We were invited to go to New York City so I would be available for auditions. My parents prayed and asked God to make a way for us to go. They wanted to hear him clearly to be sure this was something he wanted us to do.

One of our friends from church used to live in New York City, so we asked him if he knew of an inexpensive place to rent for six weeks. He talked to one of his friends who was single and living alone. This sweet lady opened her home to us, even though we were complete strangers, and let us stay with her. We were happy to sleep on the floor, because we knew God had answered our prayers and made a way for us to be there.

Our time in New York City was not what we had hoped it would be. I only had one audition and we were told I wasn't getting roles because of my southern accent. We were super disappointed, but when we went back home, we started packing. My parents were so dedicated to making my dream a reality that they decided we were moving to California. They didn't know when or how we'd get there, but they were willing to change their entire lives for me. If you haven't already guessed it, I have the most amazing parents in the world!

I was six years old when we left our comfortable lives in Mississippi and set out on a long, rough journey. All we had was faith, a promise from God, and a little bit of money. We were only in Los Angeles for two months when I booked my first role on a national AT&T commercial. I had just enrolled in an improv class at a studio, and my teacher saw my natural sense of humor. She helped me get an audition for the commercial, and I was overjoyed when I booked it! It went so well that they booked me for two more AT&T spots. Getting to do those commercials gave me so much motivation that I wanted to keep going. I was hoping to get a TV or movie role soon, of course, but that didn't happen right away. I didn't give up, though, because I believed God had more opportunities for me and I just had to be patient.

As I continued working on my acting career, I also started my singing career. I wrote and released my first single, "Win Now," when I was seven. This song is about being okay with yourself, even if you are not fitting in with the crowd. It's about believing you will win because you know God loves you and has a plan for you. This was the message I believed as I kept working toward my goal of landing a TV role, and I still keep my mind focused on this message today.

After many disappointments and lots of rejection, I finally booked the role of Judy Cooper when I was eight years old. This was the opportunity I had been hoping and praying for! I got this role exactly five days before our second-year anniversary of leaving Mississippi. My dreams were coming true, and I was super excited!

Since then I've had a lot of other high points. I preached my first sermon at our church, adopted my dog, Ginger Paris France, and sat on the panel for Girl Talk at a MegaFest conference. I feel like I am just getting started with my dreams and living my destiny. I can't wait to see the rest of what God has planned for me.

SO LET'S TALK ABOUT YOU

If you're reading this book, that means you're one of my supporters, and I want to say thank you! The first thing you should know is that when I think of you and the other people who support my work, I don't think of you as just "fans." You really are supporters, and I'm so grateful for the ways you encourage me and help me do my best!

You may be sitting with this book on your couch on a snowy day, or maybe you're close to the beach and can see palm trees out your window. You may be a kid or an adult. You may live in a country far away and come from a completely different background or ethnicity than me. That's how blessed I am—that I have this incredible group of people all over the world who support me! And the coolest thing about writing this book is that some readers may be meeting me for the very first time. No matter who you are, I'm so glad we found each other.

Even though we may have everything or nothing

in common, I love that we have the opportunity to connect with each other. One of the things I appreciate the most about my supporters is how they stick up for me online. We all know things can quickly get ugly on social media. There are always internet bullies who want to attack people. But when that happens to me, my supporters stick up for me, and it helps so much! I love how loyal my supporters are—and that includes you! Even when I'm trying to conquer something completely new (like parasailing or zip-lining), my supporters always post something to encourage me to keep going. When I meet people in person and see the joy on their faces, it encourages me to keep doing exactly what I'm doing and keep being ME!

There are a lot of ways I get to connect with my supporters. One of my favorite ways is playing online trivia games each month. I ask questions about things people know about me and it's a blast! I also ask questions about the Bible to encourage my supporters to open it and read it for themselves. The winners at the end of each game are mailed prizes. You might have seen one of my live videos on Instagram that I post each week. This is a cool way to talk to everyone because we chat about our favorite subjects in school, food, and whatever else comes to mind.

I'm so thankful that you are one of my supporters. Getting to bring you laughter and encouragement is one of the main reasons I do what I do. I hope as we go through this book together, you can see me as one of your friends—someone who understands a lot of your feelings and the things that matter to you. I am thankful for the people God has put in my life to encourage me, and I hope I get to be one of those people for you. You have a story to tell, just like I do. Keep doing the things you love and make them a part of your story. And keep telling your story to the people around you. They want to hear it!

SOME OF MY FAVORITE THINGS

1. Karaoke
2. Coloring and painting
3. Shoes
4. Traveling
5. Baking
6. The beach
7. Salad
8. Jumping on hotel room beds
9. The color pink
10. Prank calls (to family and friends)

SOME OF MY NOT-SO-FAVORITE THINGS

1. Matching socks
2. Pimples
3. Asparagus
4. Cleaning up dog poop
5. Clowns
6. The color black
7. Homework
8. Being frightened
9. Hot weather
10. Getting wet (except when I'm swimming)

FAN Q & A

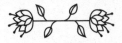

Q: What did you like most about playing a robot in K.C. Undercover?

A: My favorite part of playing a robot was all the cool stunts I had a chance to experience. Judy had her head snatched off, eyes popped out, leg pulled out, and so many other cool things. She even got a chance to drive around the ring of fire and blow fire from her mouth.

• • • • • • •

Q: What is your biggest accomplishment so far?

A: My biggest accomplishment has been writing this book because it's always been one of my dreams. This is a great way to pour into so many people and include them in my journey.

Q: Do you miss living in Mississippi?

A: No, I don't miss living there, maybe because I left when I was six years old. We have family and friends that visit us in California each year and we visit Mississippi once a year too. Sometimes I do miss the good soul food though. When my grandma (my mom's mom) comes to visit, she always cooks my favorites. Yummy!

• • • • • • • •

Q: Do you have a boyfriend?

A: No, I don't have a boyfriend because I am WAYYY too young. My "boyfriend" would be my homework study cards! My focus is on my relationship with God, school, and my career. Even if I were old enough, I don't have time for a boyfriend.

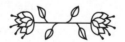

CHAPTER 2

Girl on a Mission

BEHIND THE SCENES

I've had dreams and goals for as long as I can remember, and I'm not waiting until I grow up to see them come true! Whenever a new dream or goal comes to mind, the first thing I do is write it down. Then I tell my parents. My parents always want to know my plans and goals, so they can help me accomplish them. Before we start down a new path, we pray and ask God to give us clear direction. Then we do research. Sounds crazy, I know, but sometimes you have to do homework on your dreams! We search the internet to find out exactly what it takes to accomplish what I want to do. After the research, I come up with my own personal plan and set smaller goals to help me reach my main goal. For example, when I was only six years old, I decided I wanted to be a fashion designer. I loved the idea of being different and starting my own fashion trends. My parents and I researched ways that I could learn how to sew on a sewing machine. We found out that I could take sewing lessons at a Joann Fabric store, so that's what I did. Learning to sew was the first step toward reaching my goal of being a fashion designer.

Besides writing down my goals and doing research, I also speak my list of goals out loud. If God has placed a desire in my heart, then I speak it back to him. I believe that God will help me accomplish my goals if he is the one who placed the desire in my heart. Sometimes saying the words—even if it's just to my reflection in the mirror—makes them feel more real than if I had kept those words in my head. But of course, speaking goals out loud doesn't make them happen overnight. You also need faith, discipline, consistency, and lots of prayer.

I've learned to be patient while I work on accomplishing my goals. Sometimes things happen quickly, and sometimes they don't. Remember how I told you it took almost two years for me to get the role as Judy on *K.C. Undercover?* Those were tough years. But I'd done my homework, I'd asked for God's help, and finally, my big dream came through . . . and then some! The Lord blessed me with that role even though I didn't have any TV experience. I was two years younger than what the producers were looking for, but they chose me! I was overjoyed to achieve this goal, and it taught me to trust God and his timing. As I work toward more goals and dreams in the future, this experience will give me the confidence to keep moving forward, knowing that God is in control.

I have many other short- and long-term goals, but here are a few: I would love to have my own TV show and to star in some major motion pictures. I also want to travel the world, performing my music and selling out arenas. I would love to perform on Broadway since I enjoy being on stage. And some day, I hope to walk into a department store and see my clothing line on the racks.

My advice to you is to believe you can accomplish whatever dream you have if that's what God wants you to do. Even if it looks impossible or seems too big, believe and keep working toward that dream. Stay focused, be patient, and don't give up. Sometimes we doubt ourselves or we feel like we don't know where to start—that's where planning for your dream comes in! My mom was in the military, and she's all about discipline and structure. She believes in being prepared so when an opportunity comes, you are ready for it. She has taught me to be fearless and to keep trusting God no matter what—so that's what I try to do.

SO LET'S TALK ABOUT YOU

If you're anything like me, you have LOTS of dreams you want to pursue! Since God has already helped me achieve so many of my dreams, I want to share some of the things I've learned to help you on your own journey. Girls like us dream big and have goals that can make a difference, so let's talk about the pros and cons of wanting to change the world when you're a kid.

Chasing your dreams when you're a kid can feel intimidating. But when you have a relationship with God, he will help you do everything he wants you to do, no matter what age you are or where you come from. The Bible says that nothing is impossible with

God (Matthew 19:26). With God you don't have to chase your dreams alone, and you can grow closer to him along the way.

The best way to start working toward your goals is to ask God what he wants you to do. Just keep praying for God to put his desires in your heart and he will show you what he wants for you. It makes me so happy that I get to do what I love, but it wouldn't mean anything if God's hand wasn't in it. The best part of pursuing my dreams is knowing that I'm working for him.

Another pro of being a world-changer is the chance to work with supportive adults in your life. For me, my parents are my main source of support. They have been there every step of the way, and they actually help me shape my dreams and decide which goals are best for me to pursue and which aren't. Once you have a clear dream and desire from God, I encourage you to find a trustworthy adult who can help you work toward it. Maybe for you it's your parents, or maybe it's a teacher, coach, relative, or leader at your church. Whoever it is, if this person is outside your family, make sure the other adults who care about you approve of this person.

Working with adults helps you gain important wisdom and knowledge from the experience in their lives. They can also protect you as you work toward your goals, making sure you go about it in the right way (like how my parents help me look up stuff on the internet so I stay safe online). It's really cool to have the guidance of adults, working as part of your team. And when you reach a milestone or accomplish a goal, someone is there to share the excitement with you!

Being around adult actors and other grownups in Hollywood, I've found that kids have something adults don't always have—we are fearless when it comes to dreaming big! As kids, we are learning how big the world is and how many possibilities are out there for us. We set our sights high and aren't afraid to think of crazy big goals (like getting the lead in a TV show or winning an Oscar). But sometimes, when adults face disappointments and criticism, they lose the excitement they had as kids and are scared or hesitant to chase their dreams. This is another pro of going after big goals as kids—we are courageous! Don't get me wrong, I've had my share of closed doors and being turned down, and you might too. But we have the enthusiasm to keep going and never give up. And that's what I encourage you to do!

One more pro about dreaming big as a kid is

we look at the world with fresh eyes. Sometimes, adults are so used to seeing things one way that they can't even imagine something different! But people like you and me can use our creativity to solve a problem or make a change in an entirely new way! No one else's mind works just like yours, so keep on dreaming!

Now, I'll be totally honest—it's not always easy to pursue your goals as a kid. There are definitely cons! One of the hardest things for me is that I often get left out of experiences or opportunities because I'm so young. For example, I get invited to events and parties that aren't always the best places for a young girl to be. A lot of times I can't get in because of my age or my parents won't allow me to attend because of the environment. It can be disappointing, but I know it's the best thing for me right now. And besides, attending events isn't one of my goals, it's just something that goes along with being in the entertainment industry. That might happen to you too. Maybe your dreams involve being a scientist or a doctor, and there may be events you would love to attend but they're only for adults. Remember that someday you will be able to go to those events, and until then there is still plenty you can do.

Two more cons on the list are that kids may be

limited in how many things we can pursue and the amount of time we can give to our dreams. I'm really interested in women's rights issues and in politics for example, but my parents limit how much I am involved in these areas right now. I must balance my schoolwork and other responsibilities.

It can be frustrating when people think kids like us can't change the world or that we don't know certain things. We may not have the experience of someone who is fifty years old, but kids our age are making a difference and are socially aware. If you are feeling limited in pursuing certain dreams or in the amount of time you can devote to your goals, just be patient. Chances are as you get older, your abilities and time will grow with you, and you'll be able to do things the way you want.

Chasing your dreams and changing the world are like any other experience in life—you must take the good with the bad, be sure of who you are, and surround yourself with good people who love you. With God, prayer, hard work, and the right support, anything is possible. So, my advice is: dream big!

DREAMIN'

Now that I've shared some of my dreams with you, here's space for you to think about yours. Use the questions below to help you get started or feel free to write whatever comes to mind!

1. Spend a couple of minutes praying to God. Ask him to clear your mind from distraction and help you to hear him. In the space below, write a prayer to God asking him to put his desires for your life in your heart.

2. Make a list of three to five things that you are good at, excited about, or have always wanted to do. Don't hold back anything just because it seems too big—write down whatever comes to mind!

3. Pick your two favorites from the list and fill in the blanks below. (See example for help.)

Dream 1

A goal I'd like to achieve in this area in the next year is...

Some things I need to do to achieve this goal are...

Someone who can help me work toward this goal is...

Dream 2

A goal I'd like to achieve in this area in the next year is...

Some things I need to do to achieve this goal are...

Someone who can help me work toward this goal is . . .

Example: You are talented as a singer or have always wanted to sing on stage

A goal I'd like to achieve in this area in the next year is to perform a song in front of an audience in a talent show or another event (church program, musical, etc.).

Some things I need to do to achieve this goal are research the type of event I want to sing at and find out when it takes place and how to get involved; take voice lessons or work with a music teacher at school; practice singing several days a week.

Someone who can help me work toward this goal is my piano teacher, the music teacher at school, the choir director at church.

4. Once you've narrowed down your two goals, share them with a trustworthy adult in your life. Continue to pray for God to show you what he wants you to do and keep setting smaller goals along the way to help you get to the big one.

FAN Q & A

Q: What inspires you today and how do you keep negativity away?

A: What inspires me is the fact that people look up to me and I want to make sure that I am a good example for them to follow. One way I keep negativity away is to make sure I am not hanging around with negative people.

• • • • • • •

Q: What keeps you motivated?

A: What keeps me motivated is the impact I make on people's lives. Every so often, a supporter lets me know that something I said or did was an encouragement to them. That means so much to me and makes me want to keep going when I get discouraged.

Q: What is one of the greatest challenges you've had to face, and how did you overcome it?

A: One of my greatest challenges has been geometry! I just could not understand it at first. The way I overcame it was to get a good tutor.

CHAPTER 3

Lights, Camera, Life

BEHIND THE SCENES

My life as an actress means I get to play a lot of different characters. I try to become the character when I play a role so my performance feels real, but at the end of the day, it's just a character. I need to remember that the character only lives on stage or on the screen. People often ask if there are similarities between the characters I play and who I am in real life. Sometimes there are, but not always. The characters I play might be totally awesome, or they might have traits, actions, or words that are different from how I'm being raised. The important thing for me is to make sure I keep letting my true self shine no matter where I go or what role I play.

I'm so grateful that my role as Judy Cooper on *K.C. Undercover* has given me a chance to learn about the craft of acting, build a TV family, and have a job I love. Acting is serious business, but we manage to have lots of fun too. Whenever the entire family is together in a scene, it's nonstop laughter! We always end up singing some crazy song or having a dance party in between takes. One time our director told me to recite my lines as if I were an old-time Baptist preacher. Kamil, who plays my brother Ernie, would say his lines and I would preach mine. The cast was laughing and waving their hands in the air. It turned out to be a hilarious *K.C. Undercover* "church service" and a moment I will never forget.

I love working with my TV family. I don't have any real-life siblings, so Zendaya is like an older sister to me. She always tells me that we have a voice and we need to use it for good. That's one of the most important lessons I've learned so far, and one that all of us should remember whether we feel like we're in the spotlight or in the shadows.

And trust me—I know a thing or two about feeling like I'm not number one. As an actress, I get

to attend some pretty exciting events, but I'm not always the one in the spotlight. One time I was on the red carpet doing interviews for a big movie premiere. I had just gotten to one of the media outlets when a more popular star arrived. The media people pushed me to the side and told me I had to wait because this other celebrity was coming. It was a very hard moment for me, but I learned that I will not always be in the spotlight and need to be okay with that. Sometimes my hardest moments become the times I learn the most.

I will never forget being backstage at my first Radio Disney Music Awards show! The cast from KCU was presenting an award, so we were waiting behind the stage with other presenters. A well-known celebrity was also waiting with us. When she turned around to walk on stage, she hit me with her rear end! Of course, she didn't do it on purpose, and since I am a little on the shorter side, she didn't even see me. The funny thing is that she had no idea this happened! Maybe one day I'll tell her.

Even though there are ups and downs to being an actress, the part that is always amazing is the way people have supported my career. Millions of people know who I am, even though I do not know them. It's like I have millions of friends I've never met.

That's why I love the chance to do personal appearances—to meet some of my supporters. I want them to get acquainted with the real Trinitee.

Once at an event in Florida, a little girl told me that it was her birthday and the only thing she wanted was to meet me. I talked with her for a few minutes and then we took some pictures. As they were walking away, her mom whispered to my mom that they were having a small birthday party in the hotel lobby and wondered if I could show up to surprise her. It just so happened we were staying in the same hotel, so it worked out for me to go to her party and say hi. Those are the moments I love—being able to make someone smile just by being there.

Another time, when I was meeting fans in the Midwest, a lady came to my event with her two girls. They wanted to have their picture taken with me, so I posed for a few phone pictures. Then I gave each of them an autographed photo. The mother asked if she could have one for her son since he was not able to come. She explained that her son had cancer and was not feeling well that day. She asked how much longer we would be there, and my dad told her about thirty minutes. She replied, "Well, maybe he'll be able to see you the next time you come to town."

As we were getting ready to leave, the mom returned with her seven-year-old son who was wearing a surgical mask. The boy's eyes got as big as baseballs when he saw me. He asked me to sign his hat and T-shirt. He also gave me one of his T-shirts that said he was fighting cancer. I just wanted to hug him and let him know that God is a healer. That day was very important to me, and I think about it often. It reminds me that I can share my faith and be an inspiration to others.

I know that being a young celebrity gives me opportunities that I might not otherwise have. One of the biggest highlights of my life was being invited to the Easter Egg Roll at the White House while President Obama was in office. It was a very special moment when my family and I got to meet the First Family. With tears in his eyes, my dad shared that he used to watch reruns of news clips of the Kennedy children playing in the rose garden when they were featured on TV. To see me playing with the First Lady in that same rose garden was an overwhelming blessing for him. Being able to bring joy to my dad that day is something I will always remember. Through these stories and more, I have come to realize that God has given me a unique platform both on and off the stage. I want to keep my focus

on loving others the way that God loves me, so that I can use my platform to honor him.

SO LET'S TALK ABOUT YOU

You may not have the opportunity or desire to be on a TV show, or perform on a stage in front of thousands of people, but did you know that you're in the spotlight too? It doesn't matter if you're as famous as Beyoncé or if most kids at school don't know your name—people are watching. I truly believe that our actions speak louder than words. We can influence others and change the world simply by letting God do good things through us.

You might be having an ordinary day at school, church, or participating in a club and suddenly find yourself in the spotlight. Maybe you are an excellent student and your tests or papers are shared in front of the class. Maybe you get to read a Bible verse in church on Sunday. Or maybe you're in the drama club and your idea is chosen for the next school performance. When you're in situations where attention is on you, you have two choices. You can take the glory for yourself, or you can give glory back to God.

What does that mean? Taking glory for yourself

happens when you're prideful or brag about your accomplishments and opportunities. It's okay to know your strengths and talents and celebrate them, but it's important to know we are all equal and gifted in different ways. Giving glory back to God means you are humble and thankful. You have a good attitude and work hard, even when people aren't looking. You see yourself as a team player and do your part with all your heart, no matter how big or small it is. Whenever you find yourself in a spotlight situation, pray for God's help. Tell him that you want him to have the glory and you want to show people his love.

There may be other special moments when you get to use your talents in BIG ways, like sports, music, and art. If you're a talented athlete, singer, or artist, you will probably get attention from kids and adults. In these situations, remember the Bible says to do everything for the glory of God (1 Corinthians 10:31). When you win a big game, hit the high notes perfectly, or create a masterpiece, remember who gave you the ability to do such awesome things. When people comment on your talents, you can share God's blessing with them. Using your talents is also a way to serve people around you. If you're good at sports, maybe you can help with a summer camp teaching other kids the game you love. If you are a gifted musician, maybe you can play for the elderly in retirement homes or help with a worship group at church. If you are a painter, you can participate in creating a mural to beautify your city or make valentines for people who are sick.

It's good to keep asking yourself, "How does God want me to use this talent for others?" Sometimes that looks like encouraging people on your team, in your band, or in your art class. Other times it looks like being kind and positive whether you're exceling or struggling. The important thing to remember is that your talents aren't just about you—they're about making a difference.

Another thing about being in the spotlight is at some point we all have to share it. It doesn't matter if you're the most talented person out there or you're still looking for your area to shine. There will be times when other people get the attention and praise. It's easy to feel jealous when that happens, but the best thing to do is be supportive. When other people win the award you wanted or get the lead in the play, being supportive means congratulating them with a happy heart and encouraging them as they work toward their goals.

When you believe in the destiny God has for

your life, you have the freedom to be excited for others because there is room for their destiny too. It's okay to feel disappointed when things don't go the way you wanted. But those feelings don't have to take away the joy you have for other people's success. As you encourage others in their big moments, you get to be a part of their success. And sometimes that's the most important role you can play!

So, no matter if you're in the spotlight or working backstage, remember that there is always an important job to do. Whether the whole world is watching or just your parents, God is paying attention and he cares about the way you use your talents. Always remember his opinion is the one that matters most.

Backstage Secrets of the TV Business

1. A lot of stunts are done by body doubles—
   even though it looks like your favorite
   character is doing them. My first body double
   was a man! They couldn't find a female adult
   that was my height and complexion.
2. TV makes people look bigger than they are in
   real life. When people meet me, they tell me
   I'm much smaller in person.
3. If an actor forgets his or her lines or coughs in
   the middle of a scene, we have to do it over
   until the actor gets it right. This can be funny
   or frustrating depending on the situation. It's
   hard when everyone has to start over because
   one person messes up. Sometimes a coach or
   cast member will help the actors remember
   their lines.
4. Time spent on my hair and makeup is short for
   a show like *K.C. Undercover*. Makeup can take
   longer for actresses who are adding things
   like lashes and eyebrows. Wardrobe is usually
   very quick unless you're me! I absolutely love

fashion and always want to strut down the hallway in Veronica and Tammy's high heels. (Tammy plays my mom on the show and Veronica plays K.C.'s friend Marisa.)

5. The houses on TV sets only have three walls. The fourth wall is missing because that's where the cameras and producers are.

FAN Q & A

Q: What was your first audition like?

A: My first audition was in New Orleans for a Maxwell House commercial. We got up early in the morning and drove three hours to New Orleans. I was REALLY nervous. But I was able to calm down and enter the room and own it.

• • • • • • •

Q: Was there ever a time that you were disappointed about not getting a role?

A: Yes, a few years ago I was up for this movie. It had some very well-known actors in it. I had good callbacks and everything, yet I did not book the role. I was so heartbroken and disappointed. But after the movie came out, my parents went to see it. They were disgusted with the content and happy that I wasn't in the movie. That helped me feel a little better. LOL.

Q: What was your first reaction when you found out you would be on K.C. Undercover?

A: I filmed a commercial that day. When I got home my mom told me to sit down and tell her about my day. Then out of the nowhere she screams, "You booked it!" I screamed, cried, and fainted on the floor. At that very moment, I was overcome with emotion. The thing that we came to California for was manifested.

• • • • • • •

Q: How was it working with Zendaya, and what did you learn from her?

A: It was fun working with Z. One of the most important things I learned from her was to use the voice that I have been given for good. I have also learned that your dreams can come true if you work hard.

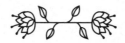

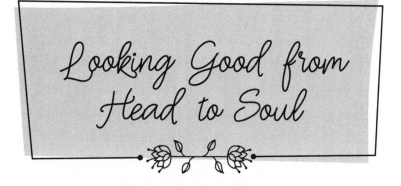

CHAPTER 4

BEHIND THE SCENES

When I was chosen for the role of Judy on *K.C. Undercover*, my first appointment was with the make-up, hair, and wardrobe experts. Since I love everything that has to do with glamour and fashion, this is the fun side of being in the industry. At my age, of course, make-up is only for special occasions like carpet events, photoshoots, or when I'm on the set. At first, I begged my parents to let me wear false eyelashes, but they said no. Now that I'm a little older, they allow me to wear them for special events, but they are almost the same length as my real lashes, so I still look my age. My parents like to remind me that I'm still a young girl and need to look like one.

I love trying different hair styles. Since my hair is thick and healthy, I can do lots of things with it. I can straighten it if I want to or just wake up and go with a natural afro. It all depends on my mood and how much time I have to style it. To keep it healthy, I use special products to wash and condition my hair and to get out the tangles. I also use essential oils and castor oil to moisturize my hair and help it grow. My mom often helps me style my hair, but when I need something different, like an up-do, I have our own hairstylist do it.

My favorite hairstyle is my natural 'fro, but my best go-to style is my natural twist out. It's the quickest style I can wear, especially on days when I rush from the set to the airport. I also love wearing my hair in individual braids, which are fun and flexible to style. I can create a lot of different looks with those braids! But styling with braids takes a little more time, so it's something I like to do on days when I'm not as busy.

People seem to be intrigued with my hair, and for some reason they want to touch it. Styling my hair can take a lot of time, and that's my personal space, so it's frustrating when people do that. I made up my own version of the song "Don't Touch My Hair" that I sing to Zendaya when we're on set. It's a sisterly thing that we laugh about because she loves to play with my hair. But she also touches it to make sure my hair is in place and protected against heat damage from curling irons and flat irons. I just wish people I hardly know would respect my personal space.

When it comes to clothes and fashion, I love creating and wearing my own designs. I came up with the idea to make my own clothes after many frustrating shopping trips. I could never find anything that I liked, and nothing seemed to fit the way I wanted it to. I love lots of color and sparkles and wanted that to be part of my personal style. I decided the only way to have clothes that reflect who I am would be to make them myself.

My mom signed me up for sewing classes, and I started with the basics. The first thing I sewed was a pillow case, then I graduated to a pair of pajamas and a tote bag. The tote bag was so cute, a few of our family members ordered some. After learning the basics of sewing, I enrolled in a private sewing class to work on clothing designs from my own sketches.

I made my first two outfits at the same time by rotating the days that I worked on each piece. One of them is a cute, colorful cocktail dress. The top of the dress is orange and shaped into a half moon with one strap that goes across the back. The bottom of the dress has multicolored stripes. The fabric flows whenever I walk or turn around, and the wide belt makes the dress look great with a pair of cowgirl boots.

The other design was a two-piece retro casual outfit. The top has hand-sewn flowers that match the pants. One leg is long with a bell bottom flare and the other leg ends right below the knee. These two outfits are special to me because they were my first fashion projects.

My parents enjoy the different aspects of fashion as well, and one year my dad designed an outfit for me to wear to the Radio Disney Music Awards. The outfit was a lime green romper with a bedazzled embellished shoulder. I was surprised at how great it turned out—it was absolutely gorgeous! I got tons of compliments on my outfit and felt like I lit up the carpet. But after a while I realized that when I hugged friends, they got a face full of sparkles! I soon figured out I needed to hug with the opposite side. My dad said it was "boy proof!"

For everyday outfits, I like colorful tights with a sparkly top. Color lives within me, so I like to wear it on the outside too. I'm also into skinny jeans with a pair of wedges. For lounging around the house, I wear oversized sweaters and sweatpants.

Even though I love fashion and care about looking good on the outside, I know it's what's inside that counts. I work on fashion as self-expression, but never want what's on the outside to get more attention than what's on the inside. It's important to let yourself shine through no matter what you're wearing.

SO LET'S TALK ABOUT YOU

The best piece of beauty advice I can give you is if you want to look gorgeous on the outside, your inside needs to mirror that. The things that make you beautiful on the inside are a loving heart and good character. When we love God, he changes our inside to be stunning. We become more patient, kind, generous, joyful, filled with peace, and humble. That's what makes a girl beautiful in every way.

Your love for God makes a difference in the way

you treat those around you. People know they can depend on you to have integrity and show the kind of love Jesus shows. Being filled with this kind of character gives you hope to see the brighter side of things and makes you more optimistic. Being a positive person filled with joy makes you attractive in a soulful way. That's the kind of beauty that never fades.

As much as I love fashion and looking good on the outside, outer beauty is much different from inner beauty. Outer beauty fades, but inner beauty lasts a lifetime. When I was much younger my grandma told me, "If you're ugly on the inside, you're ugly on the outside." It was a funny comment she made that I will never forget because it helps me balance inner and outer beauty.

The best decision we can make when it comes to beauty is to put our love for God before clothes and makeup. It's so fun to get likes and shares when you post a super cute outfit on social media, but respecting and honoring God will bring you a different kind of satisfaction that lasts forever.

I love the description of a certain woman in the Bible (Proverbs 31:10–31). We don't know her name, but she is a true fashionista. She wears gorgeous gowns made from expensive fabrics. She's also a fashion designer and sells her latest creations to retailers. But she is known for much more than her amazing style. She has such good character, you can see it on the outside. The Bible says she wears strength and self-esteem as if they were clothes. She is kind and hardworking and speaks with great knowledge. That's how she is known and remembered—not because of her pretty outfits, even though she does look good.

This chapter of the Bible clearly shows the difference between inner and outer beauty. It helps us see that there is nothing wrong with having fun expressing your style and taking care of your outer appearance, but who you are on the inside is what matters most of all.

As you continue to learn more about inner beauty, it's important to embrace your uniqueness. Loving yourself as you are—with or without all the stylish clothes and glam—is the key to feeling beautiful.

Since I'm on TV, people expect me to look a certain way and be a certain size. A lot of people make fun of my size because I'm a little bigger than most actresses my age. When I first got that reaction, it was tough for me. But then my mom helped me realize that different people prefer different body types. While some people may put me down, other people might admire my body type. I love me and my body no matter what people think. I embrace my curves and feel comfortable in my own skin.

It's important for you to embrace who you are too, both inside and out. Everything about you is unique and purposeful. You can be confident in your body and soul because you are wonderfully made by the hand of God.

How to Create My Natural Twist out 'Fro

This way of doing hair is a family tradition. My aunt Jerri taught my mom how to do this when I was much younger. This is a great hairstyle to involve your mom, sisters, aunts, whoever! I love that this hairstyle needs teamwork to create! (Hint: You might be able to find some online tutorials if you need to see someone else doing this, but also read the steps below since some of this is unique to my family.)

1. Start by washing and conditioning your hair really well with your favorite shampoo and conditioner.
2. Use a detangling product if necessary to help comb it through.
3. Apply a leave-in conditioner to make sure your hair has moisture. (You may need help from a grown-up with this step.)
4. Blow dry your hair partially, but make sure it's still damp.
5. Oil your scalp with coconut oil (you may need help from a grown-up with this step).

6. Have your mom or another grown-up part your hair into sections.

7. Spray the smaller sections of your hair with a product to lock in moisture, then apply twisting cream to each section.

8. Plait (braid) the root of each section and then twist the ends.

9. Coil the ends of each section with a comb.

10. Let your hair air dry overnight to set it, or sit under a dryer.

11. Take down each section and you will have a pretty twist out.

12. After about two days this makes your hair really big, which is the way I love it! Big hair, don't care!

How to Create My Everyday Comfortable Outfit

Since I love fashion so much, I don't believe I should sacrifice style for comfort. I love putting together cute outfits even when I have a day off from the set or I'm spending the day at home. Here are some tips to achieve a relaxed, fashionable look like mine.

Select a cute pair of tights/leggings or skinny jeans:

- For tights/leggings, I prefer fun colors like light pink or fuchsia.
- For skinny jeans, I like pairs that aren't plain, but have some type of texture or pattern. (modest rips/holes, polka dots, etc.)

Pair your bottoms with a sparkly, oversized top that complements the color of the bottoms:

- When I wear bright and bold leggings/jeans, I like to wear a more neutral-colored top. (for example, a black sparkly top with fuchsia leggings; a rose or cream-colored top with light pink skinny jeans)
- When I wear regular denim or neutral-colored bottoms, I like to wear brighter colors on the top, (for example, a coral top with polka dot denim skinny jeans; a bright pink top with black tights.)
- Look for tops that have something interesting about them: sparkles, a unique logo or saying, or a cool detail that you don't find on all shirts (like an asymmetrical shape or an interesting trim.)

Last, but most importantly, choose a fabulous pair of shoes:

- Shoes are my favorite accessory, so I always pick a pair that are fun and noticeable.
- In my opinion pink goes with everything! I wear pink shoes with pretty much any color, and I especially love pink high-top sneakers.
- I love to wear athletic shoes when I'm in a casual outfit so I can be comfortable. When I'm feeling a little sassy and the weather is right, I like to wear a pair of low wedges.

Journey with me into a world of color, sparkle, and confidence!

FAN Q & A

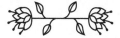

Q: Who is your fashion inspiration?

A: My fashion inspiration is Lady Gaga. I might not always agree with what she is wearing but I love the fact that she totally wears what might not be popular and owns it. Beyoncé is another fashion inspiration. She loves to take risks and I would wear almost everything she wears when she performs.

• • • • • • •

Q: How do you get your hair so poufy?

A: When my hair gets wet it literally goes wild after I blow it dry. Another way is to braid it up and let it flow.

• • • • • • •

Q: Do you have any pet peeves?

A: Yes, one of them is chipped nail polish. Another one is when I am eating at a restaurant, and someone asks to take a picture when they can clearly see that I have food in my mouth.

CHAPTER 5

For the Famous One

BEHIND THE SCENES

The one thing I know about my talents is that they are gifts God gave me before I was even born. I know that God has given me a unique platform for a reason and a purpose. He is doing big things in my life because of who *HE* is. It's not about me.

Doing commercials, recording music, and being an actress on a TV show is very exciting. But in this business, it's easy to become prideful and to feel entitled. I don't ever want that to happen to me. I am not any better than the next person—I have just been blessed with exceptional opportunities. I appreciate my friends and family members who love me for who I am and not for what I do. I spend as much time as I can with my friends and family who simply enjoy being with me.

Remaining grateful is the key to staying humble and grounded. It's something I consistently try to do. I remind myself of the sacrifices and struggles my parents had to go through to help me fulfill my dream of being on a TV show. I know there are other kids who have talents and dreams too, but their parents might not be willing or able to take a risk or make the kind of commitment that my parents are willing to make. I'm so grateful for everything my mom and dad have done to help me reach my goals. My parents have taught me to give thanks for everything, the good and the bad, because we learn from both. I call my dad the "King of Life Lessons." He believes every experience is a life lesson, and we need to be grateful for each opportunity.

Being humble helps me to respect others and treat them with kindness. Just last year I was asked to fly out of state to spend the day with a brave girl who was suffering from a liver disease. We drove up in a big Hummer limo to surprise her. We had a tea party, lunch, and ice cream, and we spent the entire

day together. She was super excited that I came to hang out with her. It's opportunities like this that are better than fame—when I get to love people in the name of Jesus and share my blessings with them.

Even though my acting career and schoolwork keep me busy, I try to make time for volunteering to help kids who are not as fortunate as I am. I enjoy organizing book drives and reading books to children. Seeing the smiles on their faces makes every minute worthwhile. I've also adopted a child through Compassion International. My financial support gives that child the opportunity to attend school and provides nourishing food and medical care. Most importantly, this child will be in a safe church environment and have many opportunities to hear about Jesus. I have been blessed, so I want to be a blessing to others.

If I'm ever tempted to be prideful about my accomplishments, I think back to an experience that humbled me to the point of tears. I was in Florida to perform at a Friday night event. I had a cute braided hairstyle, and my parents said I looked like a young Janet Jackson. Everything went well at the event, and the next day it was time to have fun. We were staying at a hotel that had a FlowRider machine. It's sort of like surfing or wakeboarding on waves that are produced by the machine. I love adventure and had always wanted to try this, so I couldn't wait to find out what it was like.

I was wearing a new swimsuit and felt like I was looking cute. I started out by lying on the bodyboard and learning how to balance it. I felt confident in that position and decided I could handle more. The person who was running the machine told me to try standing up. I thought to myself, "I've got this! I can do it!" I had seen others stand up on the board, but I had also seen a few people fall off. I figured that falling off was the worst thing that could happen, so I tried to stand up.

The power of the waves quickly knocked me off the board and pushed me toward the top of the FlowRider. I was twisting and turning in the water and finally hit the backboard. The force of the water was so strong that one of my breasts popped out! I was horrified! I covered myself and ran to my mom crying. I was not physically hurt—just humiliated. Thank goodness no one saw my exposure, and I was thankful when the whole episode was over.

My dad joked that on top of looking like Janet Jackson, I was trying to be like her, and we all laughed. But I realized through this experience that anything can happen to anyone, and I should never laugh when someone has an embarrassing moment. We all have moments that we'd rather forget. During those times we can remember how important it is to stay humble when we're flying high.

SO LET'S TALK ABOUT YOU

I am confident that the Lord put me on this earth for the entertainment industry. He is calling me to change lives and lead people to him by using my talents. All the things I believe about my personal mission are also true for you! God has given you special talents and skills to use at a very specific time and place. He wants you to feel fulfilled and alive when you do the things he's created you for. And more than that, he wants you to use your talents and opportunities to share his love with others.

It's important that we stay focused on our mission, so that we do what God wants us to do instead of what everyone else wants us to do. My embarrassing moments have shown me that success has both highs and lows. We can fall out of our successes even more quickly than we come into them. That's why it's so important to make every moment count when you're living your dream.

I encourage you to be proud of your accomplishments and own your strengths and talents. I have found that confidence is very empowering and a huge part of chasing your dreams. You must believe in yourself, because sometimes other people won't believe in you. I will always celebrate my successes and jump up and down when I win awards, but I am able to do so because God helps me keep my heart in the right place.

The best way to keep your heart in the right place is by praying and studying the Bible. These are the ways God lets you know what he wants you to do. As you learn that it's God who's writing your story, it keeps you humble and helps you treat others right. One of my favorite scriptures is Matthew 7:12: "So in everything, do to others what you would have them do to you . . ."

The two biggest parts of being humble are recognizing what others do to help you reach your goals and being willing to be a servant. Being a servant means you put others before yourself. You do things to help others before you help yourself, and you think of their feelings and needs along with your own. It's like the golden rule—do for others what you would want them to do for you.

I've shared with you how much my parents have

helped and encouraged me in all my dreams. I am always willing to brag on them because I know I wouldn't be here without them. I pray you have people like that in your life too. Today, take a couple minutes to think about a few people who have really helped you in your achievements. Maybe your math teacher tutored you and you got a good grade on one of your tests. Maybe your coach spent extra time with you to get your form just right and it made a big difference in your game performance. As you identify the people who have contributed to your growth and achievement, I encourage you to thank them (privately or publicly). Gratitude never goes out of style, and it's a great habit to start now.

Being willing to serve others means helping people just like you have been helped. Maybe one day you can go to school early to rehearse lines with someone in the play who needs extra practice. Or maybe you can buy an extra set of paints and brushes for a classmate who needs them.

Every step of my career has shown me that success is a team effort. Sometimes you're the one being supported and served, and sometimes you're the one doing the supporting. It's not about the size of your role, but the size of your heart and listening to what God tells you to do.

TEXT MESSAGE FROM TRINITEE

I want to tell you to always believe you can accomplish your dream. Even if it looks impossible or you think it's too big, still believe. Work hard and have integrity. Never let anyone discourage you about following your dreams. Always be true to yourself. There is no one else in this world that can do YOU. Last but not least, leave behind a legacy of faith.

Smooches, Trinitee

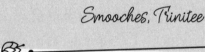

FAN Q & A

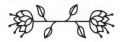

Q: How do you walk on the streets without people noticing you?

A: I don't really. A lot of people have learned my facial structure even if I am wearing sunglasses, so it is not very often that I am not recognized.

• • • • • • •

Q: How many foreign languages do you speak?

A: I am currently learning Spanish! I am going to start Latin in a couple of months. Latin will help me with the SAT.

• • • • • • •

Q: What is your favorite genre of music?

A: I listen to a lot of different styles of music. It really depends on what I am in the mood to listen to. But my all-time favorite is country music.

CHAPTER 6

BEHIND THE SCENES

I wouldn't be where I am today if it weren't for my parents. Before I was born, my mom quit her job so she could care for me and give me everything I needed. My parents have made many sacrifices to help me become all that God created me to be. The biggest sacrifice was leaving behind their life in Mississippi and moving to California for me to pursue my dreams. A lot of people thought they were crazy, but they did it anyway. My parents support me in every possible way. No matter what I want to do, as long as it is safe and appropriate for someone my age, they find a way to help me do it.

Since I'm still a minor, my parents travel with me when I go to special events. Most of the time my dad travels with me, but my mom joins us if it's something I've never done before. At an event in Houston last summer, I was a keynote speaker for the first time. Mom came along because she didn't want to miss that. It's always great to have both of my parents by my side!

My acting career keeps us very busy, so we use our free time to just hang out together as a family. We love going to the beach because the water is so peaceful it helps us rest and relax. On Fridays we have game night, and that's really fun. My mom makes homemade loaded nachos and her famous strawberry lemonade. We play games like Monopoly, Clue, Uno, and Life, and sometimes we wear wigs just to be silly. Mom is very competitive and almost *always* beats Dad and me.

My family takes a vacation every year, and we love visiting islands. One time we went to Jamaica and stayed at an all-inclusive resort with a beach and several swimming pools. We ate lots of jerk chicken and drank thirst-quenching fruity beverages. While we were in Jamaica, my parents and I went hiking for the first time. I wasn't sure I wanted to sign up for the hike, but we all got up the nerve and did it. We hiked the Dunn's River Falls with a tour group, holding hands to keep each other from falling. Water splashed on us, and it also started raining which made the rocks slippery. It was very challenging and a little scary for me, but I'm glad we did it. It's one of our best family memories.

Holidays are always a special time for me and my parents. Like many families, we have some fun traditions. During the Christmas season, we decorate gingerbread houses and dip them in hot chocolate. Then we bundle up and ride through the neighborhood to look at the beautiful Christmas lights.

Another one of our favorite family traditions is our blessings box. We write our blessings on slips of paper and put them in the box all year. Then around the holidays, we empty the box and read the slips of paper. It's a time of thanksgiving as we reflect on the good times, happy times, and sad times. It shows us how the Lord was with us throughout the year and brought us through everything we faced. We give thanks and praise to the Lord for these blessings.

We also do some silly things like singing the Christmas blues—very dramatically! And one of my favorite things we do is send voice texts to our extended family and friends. Even our dog, Ginger, gets in on the act! We sing off key and send funny or spooky messages, then wait for a response. It's hilarious! Our family and friends love it and look forward to our messages every year.

Even though I have a demanding career, my parents help me find the right balance between reaching for my dreams and being a regular girl. Spending time with my parents is what keeps me secure and grounded. I know they will always be there for me through all the ups and downs of being in the entertainment business. My parents know it's important for me to have everyday family experiences. They want me to have a wonderful childhood. After all, you only get one chance to be a kid!

SO LET'S TALK ABOUT YOU

Your family might look a lot like mine, with two parents and a dog. Or your family might be very different. Maybe you have a lot of siblings, or a farm full of animals, or maybe you live with your grandparents or an aunt. No matter what your family looks like, always remember that God puts each family together. Sometimes families come together through adoption or foster care. And sometimes families are blended with step-parents and step-siblings. Whatever your background is, I hope you can see God's hand in putting you all together and *your* purpose in being a part of it.

Always remember that *you* are an important family member—even if you are young. You fill a special place in your family that God designed just for you. Your talents, personality, strengths, and even your challenges are a part of what makes your family so wonderful and one-of-a-kind. Your family is learning from you and growing just because you're you! If there are ever days that you feel out of place, remember this: no one can be the child, sibling, grandchild, cousin, or pet parent you are. You are important, and your family is better because you are a part of it!

There are lots of great ways you can bless, support, and contribute to your family no matter how old you are or what kind of family you're a part of. One of my favorite ways of supporting my family is through prayer. Prayer is great because you can do it anytime, anywhere. It's important for every family no matter what's going on. You can even pray for your family when you live far apart!

If you haven't prayed a lot before or you're not sure how to start, here are some tips. Just think of prayer as having a conversation with God. You can tell him anything you want to say about your family (or anything else). You can ask him to keep your family safe, to provide for your family, to help your family members with specific challenges they face, and to help you love and take care of each other. I also ask God to help my family know and love him more because I think that's the most important thing of all.

Besides prayer, you can bless your family through encouraging words. You can leave a note for your mom or dad, to say thank you for all they do. You can tell your sister or your cousin what you think they are good at and where you see their talents. You can tell your grandma you love her or tell your aunt that she's doing a good job at work. Words are a powerful tool, and it's amazing to see how much a kind word can build your family members up.

Another way you can contribute to your family is by doing things to help or serve. Things like doing the dishes, taking out the trash, folding laundry, and helping take care of younger siblings or cousins are great ways to be a team player. Keeping a family going is a lot of work, and everyone can do something to help. When you do things to support your family, you show them you care, just like when one of your family members makes your favorite meal or plays a game with you.

Last but definitely not least, one of the most important jobs you have in your family is to respect your parents and follow their rules and boundaries. No matter what kind of family you have, I pray there is an adult in your life who cares about you and wants what's best for you. It may be your mom or dad, or maybe it's an aunt, uncle, teacher, or grandparent. The rules and limits adults give us are for our good, even though we might not understand them all the time.

I've realized my parents have lived a lot more life than I have and they're very wise. Our parents are usually right, even though we might not want to admit it! Listening to the adults who take care of us shows that we respect and trust them and that they can trust us too.

Your family makes you who you are, even if there are things about your family you'd like to change. God put these specific people in your life to help write your story. On the good days and the hard days, remember you're right where you're supposed to be with people who are helping you grow inside and out.

There are a lot of stories in the Bible about how God works through our families. God created the whole nation of Israel through Abraham's one son, Isaac. Joseph's brothers ganged up on him and sent him away, but later, God used Joseph to provide food for his family as well as an entire country! And Jesus' brother, James, eventually believed that Jesus was God's son and ended up writing a book of the Bible.

There is a reason why God puts each of us in a certain family. We might not always understand everything about our families, but we can trust God's plan.

FUN FAMILY ACTIVITIES

1. **Have a karaoke night!** Make popcorn and take turns belting out your favorite songs. At the end of the night, give out silly awards like "best dance moves," "best high note," and "worst song to fall asleep to."

2. **Do something nice undercover.** Pick another family or person you know and do something for them (bake cookies, drop off flowers, rake their yard, etc.). The catch: you have to do the good deed without getting caught!

3. **Celebrate a half-holiday.** Choose a holiday or birthday of someone in your family and celebrate a mini-version on the half-date (6 months after the real date; for example, half-Christmas would be June 25). Do things to make it just like the real day (bake a cake, open presents, dress up, etc.) Take pictures to document your holiday!

Activities to Do For Each Other

1. **Tablecloth notes.** Find a plain cloth or paper tablecloth (make sure it's one you can write on) and some permanent markers. Pick a family member to honor during a meal. Have all the other family members write encouraging notes and things they love about the honored family member on the tablecloth. You can take turns over the course of a few weeks so everyone gets their own tablecloth.

2. **Chore surprise.** Pick a chore that another family member usually does and do it for them when they are sleeping or not at home.

3. **Parent assistant.** Ask your parent (or another grownup who takes care of you) what you can do to help them for the day. Do the things they ask without complaining and have fun helping!

FAN Q & A

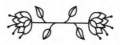

Q: What can parents do to help their kids have a close relationship with God and understand what that means?

A: Parents can read the Bible with their kids and take them to church. Something else that a parent can do is teach their children to pray which is the best way to build a relationship with God.

• • • • • • •

Q: How is it being an only child?

A: Being an only child has its pros and cons. One of the pros is that I don't have to share the attention that I get from my parents. A con would be that sometimes I get lonely.

Q: *Have you ever attended a regular school?*

A: I actually have not. I have visited a few though. My family moved from Mississippi after my kindergarten graduation. I have been homeschooled ever since then.

• • • • • • •

Q: *How do actors know when to get serious and start filming?*

A: Some actors stop playing around when the director says "action" and some people like me play in between scenes or on a break. I try to focus on the scene that I am in. I can play later.

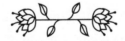

CHAPTER 7

Iron Girls

BEHIND THE SCENES

My mom has great friends. They pray and laugh together, inspire and motivate each other. Their friendship is deep and honest. They even feel comfortable letting each other know when the other is wrong. That's love, and it's the kind of friendship that makes you a better person. I've told my mom many times that I want friends like she has. I want friends who will accept me for who I am and who will encourage me to go after my dreams. My dad always tells me that I need to *be* the type of friend that I want to have. So that's what I try to do—accept my friends for who they are and encourage them to do whatever they feel God is calling them to do.

I'm thankful for the good friends I have because it's hard to make friends when you're in Hollywood. There is so much competition between young women—especially in the entertainment industry. I have a friend who auditions for some of the same roles I do. When that happens I am excited when either one of us books the role. Our parents pray together about our careers, so if one of us gets it, we see it as an answered prayer. It's important to never let being in the industry get in the way of friendship. We cheer for each other and never have hard feelings when one of us gets a role. We work hard and prepare for our auditions. We do our best to improve ourselves and sharpen our crafts. I believe I will get the opportunities that God wants me to have. If I don't get a role, then God intended it for someone else.

Having good friends can be challenging when you are living in the spotlight. That's why I feel so blessed to have awesome friends. Just like other girls my age, I love to laugh and have fun. I have friends who are triplets. We love doing crafts and artsy things together, but we also like to bake. One time our moms were watching TV and we asked if we could bake a treat. They said we could, and they were so into their show they didn't pay attention to what we were doing. We searched the cabinets and fridge and pulled out tons of ingredients. As the four of us each made a different dessert, we spilled flour and sugar all over the kitchen. After we baked our desserts, we offered our moms a taste, but they said the treats were too sweet. When they finally saw the messy kitchen, they were shocked and said we needed to clean it up. It took us just as long to clean the kitchen as it had to bake our desserts in the first place! But the best kind of friends make even boring things—like cleaning—lots of fun.

I also love hanging out with my friends who are twins. One day when I was at their house, our parents left us with our dance teacher while they went out for a while. We thought it would be fun to make dinner together. We found recipes for veggie egg rolls and potato soup on a website. Our teacher was heating oil in a skillet while my friends and I rolled the filling inside the eggroll wraps. Our teacher also started making the potato soup. We put the egg rolls in the skillet and allowed them to cook while we went to play a game. Our game was so fun that we forgot about the egg rolls and soon smelled something burning. We ran to the kitchen to find our egg rolls burned to a crisp. Then we accidentally knocked the entire container of salt into the potato soup and ruined that as well. When our parents came home, they were surprised to find out we had ruined both dishes. My mom teased our teacher and said, "I thought you knew how to cook." Our teacher replied, "Well, I guess I need to learn more." After we all had a good laugh, we ordered pizza!

Another friends' adventure happened when I was in Nashville taping an episode of Priscilla Shirer's online show "The Chat with Priscilla." After we finished taping, my parents went out for dinner with some of their friends, so I stayed at the hotel with a few of mine. We put on our pajamas and sat down inside the elevator as it went up and down between the floors. As people got on and off, they smiled at us and asked what we were doing. We giggled and said we were just going for a ride. Most of them replied, "Well, have fun!" And we sure did!

I have some great memories with my friends, and I hope to make many more. I am thankful that even though I have a busy life, God has given me friends I can hang out with. Good friends are a gift from God, and I thank him for that blessing.

SO LET'S TALK ABOUT YOU

What kinds of friends do you have? What qualities do you look for when you make new friends? A lot of times it's easy to make friends with people who share your interests (just like some of my friends are actors). But there are a lot of other qualities a good friend possesses. If you're not sure how to choose good friends, there's a Bible verse that helps me remember what to look for: "As iron sharpens iron, so one person sharpens another" (Proverbs 27:17). This verse means that the friends in our lives should make us better—and we should do the same for them.

A lot of people make popularity the goal when it comes to having friends. Everybody likes to be liked! But I've found that it's better to have a few good friends than lots of not-so-good friends. Just because you hang out with the cool kids doesn't always mean you have the right kind of friends. You need to pray for wisdom when you meet new people and ask the Lord to send you the friends that you need in your life. Those are the friendships that make a difference in your life and theirs.

You may want to hang out with certain people because they seem fun, but they might not necessarily be the ones that will help you be the kind of person you want to be. And they might pressure you to do things you know you shouldn't do. It's important to know the difference between who your true friends are and which people you just hang out with and laugh with in certain situations or events. Knowing the difference will keep you from being hurt or disappointed. I've definitely learned that lesson being in the entertainment industry and being around lots of different people in all kinds of situations.

When you think about the kind of person you want to be, seek out friends whose good traits will rub off on you. If you want to be kind and encouraging, look for those qualities in your friends. If you want to be silly and laugh a lot, look for friends who have fun! Some other qualities that make good friends are loyalty, compassion, honesty, trustworthiness, patience, and forgiveness. When you find people who are genuine and loving, it helps create friendships that build you up and give you support through thick and thin.

And just like you want a friend who is all of these things, it's important to *be* a friend like this too. Being a good friend means you are kind and helpful. You encourage your friends and are nice to them no matter what. You say you're sorry if you hurt your friends' feelings, and you forgive them if they hurt yours. You don't say mean things behind their backs, and you are honest in a loving way. You accept your friends for who they are and love them for the unique people God made them to be. Being a good friend means being there when your friends are going through a hard time. And it means being happy for your friends when good things happen to them.

There are lots of ways you can encourage and support your friends whether they're having good days or bad days. I love writing notes and sending messages to my friends. It's a way they can keep receiving encouragement. You can leave a message on their social media so other people can encourage them too!

Another way to support your friends is by going to the events they're involved in. You can go to their soccer games, piano recitals, theater productions, and math competitions. Being in the audience is a great way to show you care. You can also give them presents on their birthdays and bake them cookies just because! And if there's ever a day one of your friends is sad, you can just sit and cry with her. Sometimes just being there is the most important thing you can do.

While there are lots of things we should do to be a good friend, there are also some things we *shouldn't* do. For now, let's just talk about one big one: gossip. We can think of gossip as spreading rumors or spreading information that another person doesn't want shared. The problem with gossip is that it puts another person down or makes them look bad. That's not what a good friend does.

It's easy to get caught up in gossip, especially when other people start it. It takes a strong person to stop and say they won't be a part of it. Living in the spotlight, I've seen firsthand the harm gossip causes and how bad it can hurt. We don't make ourselves look better by making other people look bad. So, I encourage you to *never* be the person who starts gossip and to *always* be the one who stops it. That's what a true friend does.

Making friends and being a good friend isn't always easy, but it's worth it when you do it the right way. I hope as you continue to live your story you find friends who sharpen you like the Scripture says. Life can be as crazy as a rollercoaster ride, and it's nice to have someone sitting next to you through all the ups and downs.

TEXT MESSAGE FROM TRINITEE:

Hi! With my busy schedule it can be hard to keep in touch with my friends at times. But I am really committed to my friendships, so I always find ways to stay connected! Here's how I keep up with my friends. Maybe these ideas will help you stay close to your friends too!

—Email, video chatting, and texting

—Going to visit friends who live far away when I have free time

—Writing letters—when my parents feel I need a break from electronic devices, it's a fun way to keep in touch!

Smooches, Trinitee

FAN Q & A

Q: *You are always having fun with your friends. Which one of your friends is wild and crazy like you?*

A: Oh, that is a good question. All my friends are so different. But the one friend that is wild and crazy is my buddy Eris! We have tons of fun when we are together.

• • • • • • •

Q: *If you could meet any celebrity, who would it be?*

A: I can't wait to meet Chrissy Teigen because she is so awesome. She speaks her mind and is such a creative person. I would absolutely love to meet Chance the Rapper, Katy Perry, and Beyoncé too. I also want to meet Madea. LOL.

• • • • • • •

Q: *What was the first song you fully memorized?*

A: The first song I memorized and could perform was Adele's "Rolling in the Deep." It is still one of my favorites.

CHAPTER 8

Unstoppable Destiny

BEHIND THE SCENES

I've shared my goals with you, and I'm sure by now you understand that I am determined to pursue my passions and dreams no matter what. I face challenges now and then, but that doesn't stop me from doing what I believe God wants me to do. I have many wonderful supporters, and I am very grateful for them. But not everyone I meet is a supporter. That's just the way it is in this business, and I have to be okay with that. I know I'll always have people who encourage me and build me up, but there will also be those who try to bring me down.

When people tell me I can't do something, I ignore them and keep moving on. Sometimes criticism can even motivate me to work harder to achieve my goals. Over the years, I've learned the best way to rise above negativity is to be successful—and do it with a smile.

I also pray for those who are unkind to me. I realize that people who say or do hurtful things don't always intend to be that way. They might not have anyone in their lives to build them up. If they lack self-worth, then they may not have the ability to see the good in others. I pray that they will find God and discover their meaning and purpose in life. I ask God to help them on their journey.

Besides dealing with negative comments from others face-to-face, I also have to handle virtual negativity. Social media has become a powerful communication tool, and cyberbullying is a serious problem. It's important for kids to be smart and safe online so we can be protected from the dangers that are out there. My mom handles my social media accounts, so I don't spend a lot of time on the internet, and when I am online, one of my parents is nearby.

I never talk to anyone online without my parents' approval, and if I come across a suspicious or mean comment, I tell my parents right away. I love chatting with some of my industry buddies, and I would like to spend more time on social media, but I know my parents' restrictions are for my own good.

My parents usually block negative comments from my newsfeed, so I don't see them, but that doesn't protect me from everything. One time I was doing a live video on Instagram and someone told me to sit down. They said I could not sing and that I was fat and ugly. I couldn't believe people were saying mean things to me in the middle of my live video. I didn't allow their hurtful words to shake me though. I tried to rise above it and not let it get to me. Even though it was hard, I decided to stay strong and positive and respond with a smile. I told them I was praying for them and that I loved them, because sometimes bullies just need someone to show them love and attention. When they apologized I added, "I love ME just the way that I am!"

I knew people said negative things about me on social media but having this happen to me in a live video was totally different. I told my mom about it and she told me to shift my thoughts to remembering who I am and who I belong to. I immediately focused on Bible verses that tell me I am fearfully and wonderfully made, and I am the apple of God's eye. In a way, my parents were glad that incident happened because it made them realize they can't shield me from everything bad in the world. Sometimes my supporters come to my defense, and I truly appreciate that. But this experience taught me how to face adversity. I have to be able to stand up for myself under any circumstance and encourage others to do the same.

That's why, in 2017, I recorded the song "Miss Me," which has a message of empowerment and inspiration. It's about standing up for something great and being true to who you are, even if you stand alone. It talks about not letting negative words or pressure from others dictate how you should live your life. The song encourages listeners to remain focused on their purpose and destiny and dismiss anything that is different from what they know is true. The words in the song are personal to me because I want to live life unapologetically and inspire others to do the same. I hope my music will be the force that will ignite a fire inside and empower others to love.

In order for people to be strong and confident in who they are, they need to recognize their value and worth. For me, my worth comes from knowing what God thinks about me. I have a choice to believe what people say about me or believe what God says about me. I choose to believe what God says. He is the one who shapes my destiny, and nothing can stop his plans!

SO LET'S TALK ABOUT YOU

The most important part of embracing your own destiny is valuing yourself and developing your self-confidence. You have to disregard what anyone else says about you that is opposite of what you know is true. All that confidence starts with knowing your worth as a person.

I came up with some important truths that spell the word W.O.R.T.H. to help me remember my value no matter what. I hope this tool shows you how to truly love and accept yourself for the unique person God made you to be!

W stands for *wonderfully made*. The Bible says that each person is fearfully and wonderfully made by God (Psalm 139:14). That means that God has a purpose for everything you are from the inside out—even things you'd rather change about yourself. God is perfect, and he doesn't make mistakes. Everything about you is wonderfully created.

O stands for *orchestrated*, which is a fancy way of saying planned or arranged. You were carefully thought out by God. Your body type, skin color, and even your toes were designed by God. This is why I encourage you to embrace your uniqueness, even if it seems strange to others. The Lord crafted you together, like a potter sculpting clay. So, if you have chubby toes, one dimple, or no hair at all, own it with confidence!

R stands for *resilient*. Being resilient means you bounce back when you face challenges instead of letting them get you down. Like I said earlier, social media has a huge effect on us. There may be times when things you see on social media cause you to doubt yourself or make you feel pressured to do things you know aren't right. Maybe there are times when you want to try something new, but you face rejection. Maybe others bully you or call you names—pray and ask the Lord to build you back up. No one feels good all the time, but if you are resilient, you can encourage yourself to keep moving forward.

T stands for *think positive*. Thinking positive thoughts is something we all have to constantly work on. One way to maintain your confidence and self-esteem is to repeat truths about yourself every day. I created a list of things that "**I AM**" and I recite them in the mirror each day. Reciting this list motivates me and helps me feel strong. It might be helpful for you to do the same thing. Make a list of true, positive things about yourself that you can own and cling to. Saying it out loud makes it more of a reality and silences the negative voices in our heads. Also, beware of being around negative people, because negativity can be contagious. Instead, think positive thoughts and believe in yourself.

H stands for *hinder*. Never allow other people's words or actions to hold you back or weigh you down. Empower yourself with the Word of God and with knowledge. Find what makes you unique and grow that gift or talent. You are the only person who can fulfill your destiny. You are the only one who can be the best *you*. Don't allow anyone to keep you from accomplishing God's mission for you. And don't hinder *yourself* by being the one to weigh you down. Work to improve your self-esteem in the areas where you struggle. A confident person can change the atmosphere of an entire room by simply being present.

Now that you know your W.O.R.T.H., I want to

leave you with the two most powerful tools you can use to live out your identity: prayer and the Word of God. Although they are free, nothing can bring more value to your life than these tools. Prayer is the way we talk to God; God's Word is one of the ways he talks to us. As you continue to discover the truth that God loves you and has good things for you, it motivates you to keep going no matter what. Living the life God wants for you is the key to fulfilling your destiny.

MISSION STATEMENTS

Create a mission or identity statement for yourself using the guide below. Use this statement to begin claiming the truth about who you are and what you want, especially when you face criticism from others. You can repeat it daily in the mirror, write it somewhere you see it every day, or make up a tune to sing it to.

1. List your past achievements and some things you've done that you're proud of. This can be related to schoolwork, sports, arts, friendships, community service, etc. *(Examples: received a good grade on a presentation of an interesting subject, placed in a dance competition, helped feed the homeless, encouraged a friend who was hurting)*

2. List the beliefs and ideas that are most important to you, especially those that you feel define who you are. Make your list as long as you want and then circle the three that are most important. *(Examples: honesty, kindness, determination, hard work, faith, service, achievement, helping)*

3. Think of ways you can make a difference to the world, your family, your friends, or your community. (*Examples: building up your friends with kindness and encouragement, using your talent for singing or acting to bring messages of hope and help to your audience, creating a special service organization to reach people in need*)

4. Make a list of goals you'd like to achieve in the near future and distant future. Focus on the things that are most important to you and will always be a part of who you are. Refer to the goals you created in Chapter 2 for extra help. (*Examples: become a regular performer in music or dance, receive recognition for scientific research, volunteer 100 hours of community service, start a monthly friendship event to promote kindness and support between classmates*)

5. Using all the information above, write a short mission/identity statement to help you stay focused on who you are and what your destiny is. Don't forget to pray and look for

wisdom in the Bible as you do this! Here is my personal mission statement as an example to help you form yours: *To live life with integrity and impact the world using my creativity and vivacious spirit. To inspire the world to have faith and pursue destiny. To help girls and women of all ages to know their value and understand that their worth is greater than their exterior.*

FAN Q & A

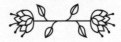

Q: As a successful individual, how do you handle the pressure of work, school, and life in general?

A: When it comes to pressure I have found a balance of having fun on the weekends and working hard during the week. Also, I love to paint and color. That relieves my pressure.

• • • • • • •

Q: If someone is having a bad day, what is one thing you would say to them?

A: I would tell them they look better when they smile and tell them a funny joke. It never hurts to give them a hug too.

• • • • • • •

Q: Are you flexible?

A: I am a little flexible. I could use some help in that area. LOL. I have tried to start stretching more so that I can increase my flexibility.

CHAPTER 9

Get Your Serve On

BEHIND THE SCENES

God blesses us in many ways. He blesses us with things we need like food and clothing, family and friends. Even sunshine and rain are blessings, though sometimes for different reasons. But another way to be blessed is to *be* a blessing to others. It makes my heart happy when I can make someone happy. My parents have always stressed the importance of serving others, and I hear that same message at church. You don't have to look far to find someone who has a need, great or small. I want to help others in any way I can. Some people need money for food, clothes, or school supplies. Many people can't afford the things they need to live a healthy life, such as toothpaste, shampoo, or cleaning supplies. A lot of things we take for granted. But I know that God has blessed me and my family with many things, so I want to be part of assisting those who might need a little extra help.

Helping people in need is a great thing to do, but serving others is more than that. Service is an opportunity to be selfless and do something good for someone else. Serving others takes the focus off ourselves and puts it on the people we serve. When you respond to someone's need, you can fill that person with so much joy that it shows on their face as a great big smile. You can brighten someone's day just by a simple act of love or kindness. Serving others keeps you humble, centered, and grateful for what you have. Plus, it just feels good. Serving others is a way to use your talents and resources to make the world a better place. It's a way we can be more like Christ and follow his example.

When we first moved to California, my parents were trying to find a way that we could be involved in service projects. My mom researched organizations and found the Ronald McDonald House.

There are more than 350 Ronald McDonald Houses in the United States. These homes provide a place where families can stay if they have a child in a hospital that is far from their own home. Families can stay there at little or no cost, and it allows them to spend as much time as possible with their sick or injured child. We got all the information on the different ways we could meet the needs of the families who stay there. We decided to fix meals for the kids and their families. We got together with some of our friends, went grocery shopping, and brought the groceries to the Ronald McDonald House in our area. Then we lit up the barbeque grill and started cooking. When the food was ready, we fixed plates and served the families a delicious meal. After dinner, I sat down and colored pictures with some of the kids staying there. It was so much fun!

For the past few years my family and I have participated in the Disney Family Day of Service Volunteer Day. Every year we do something different. One year we sorted apples from huge bins. We had to pick apples one at a time to see which ones were good and place them in a separate crate from the rotten ones. We only wanted the best apples for the families who would receive them. Another year we put together meal bags to donate. We filled bags with items that a family could use to prepare a meal. This year we are going to work with Points of Light, which is one of the largest service organizations in the world. Their mission is to have people work together to change the world through volunteerism and service.

Besides being involved in organizations, we try to think of other ways we can serve on our own. My dad came up with a super cool idea and I joined in. Being in the entertainment industry, I end up having a lot of clothes and shoes that I don't need and which I often give to my friends or relatives. But there are many times when we are out at the store or driving around and see needy families asking for money. Our hearts are really tugged when we see children out with their moms. So, my dad's idea was to put together "blessing bags." We put clothes, shoes, and hair bows in bags and keep them in our trunk. Whenever we see a mom with a girl who may have a need, we give them one of our blessing bags. After we drive away, I love to imagine that little girl wearing the clothes and clipping a cute bow in her hair.

Another thing I like to do is hold book drives so that I can help children with literacy. I collect new or used book donations. I enjoy having my picture taken with the people who donate the books, and they enjoy it too. Then we choose a few different shelters or group homes and deliver the books to the children who live there. Many of the children have been taken away from their parents because of abuse or neglect or are not with their families for many other reasons. The state provides homes where they can be safe. These might be the only books some of the children will ever have as their own, and I want every child to have access to books!

My parents and I have had many opportunities to be involved in service projects, but sometimes we just respond to something we see in the moment. One day we were walking toward our truck at Walmart when we saw a lady in a wheelchair trying to put groceries in her trunk. I asked my parents if I could help her and they said, "Of course!" At first when I walked up to her, she looked a little unsure of me. I told her that I wanted to help her, and then she agreed. After I loaded her groceries in her trunk, I gave her a hug. She was so grateful and told me I was very kind. It was something simple for me to do, but it was such a big help to her.

You've probably heard the saying that charity starts at home. Well, it's true! One time when my grandma was staying with us, we spent a lot of time walking around sightseeing and doing lots of activities. When we were at home, she complained that her feet were hurting, which gave me a great idea. I got out my foot spa and had her soak her feet in an Epsom salt bath. Then I gave her a pedicure and painted her toe nails. She was so appreciative and happy. It was a fun and simple way to show her I love her and make her feel special. Service doesn't have to be complicated! Small acts of kindness to those closest to you are some of the easiest and most important forms of giving.

These are just a few examples of the different ways that we have served others in our community and at home. Serving others is sure to bring lots of smiles—and don't be surprised if you end up wearing one too!

SO LET'S TALK ABOUT YOU

What do you think of when you think about service? Some people think that service projects are for missionaries or big organizations. Or that service is for rich and famous people to give back and promote good causes. But the truth is that everyone can and should serve others. It doesn't matter what your age or status is, you have something to offer. You don't need a lot of time or money to make a difference in someone's life. You just need to pay attention to those around you and look for ways you can offer help or assistance.

If you see a child at the park or playground with an untied shoe, take a minute to tie it! If you see an elderly person sitting on a bench, sit next to them and let them talk to you. Being a good listener can make someone feel important. You can hold doors for mothers with young children, or people on crutches, or help someone walk up the stairs who could use an extra hand. And what about that boy or girl who doesn't have many friends at school or church? You know the answer to that! Invite them to sit with you. Your neighbor might be a single parent and need some help. You can volunteer to play with the kids outside while their mom or dad prepares dinner. If you receive an allowance, you can save some of your money to donate to a local charity. The possibilities are endless when you open your eyes to the needs of those around you!

There are many reasons why it's important to serve. First, service is a practical way that you can make a difference in the world—even if it's one person at a time. Any act of kindness you show to someone matters to that person. You have no idea what the domino effect of it could be! And larger service projects allow you to make an impact that will last for years—like helping build a school on a mission trip or raising money to fight diseases. When you see how much you can give through your time and possessions, you realize how much one person *can* change the world. If we aspire to be the type of people who are loving and strong and live up to our potential, we need to grab every opportunity we have to make the world a better place!

Another great reason to get involved in service is that it builds character. Taking the time to think of others and leaving room in your schedule to be available for serving requires a lot of selflessness and thoughtfulness. Putting others before yourself doesn't always come easily, especially when you have a lot going on in your own life. But the more you practice service and make it a regular part of your life, the more natural it will feel and the more you'll want to do. You can also learn hard work, commitment, gratitude, and responsibility. These are all things that make us well-rounded people!

Service projects can also help you build a lot of practical skills through different opportunities. For example, Habitat for Humanity uses volunteers to build affordable homes for people who can't afford more expensive homes. If you volunteer to work on one of their homes, you can learn about construction and how to use different kinds of tools. If you help run a food drive, you'll gain experience with organization and management. And participating in 5K race fundraisers can help you stay physically healthy as you exercise, while giving to a good cause. Any time you serve others, your knowledge of the world will increase, and you will gain experiences and memories that you will carry into the future.

The last and most important reason it's good to serve is that it brings glory to God. Hebrews 13:16 reminds us that when we serve others, we are also honoring God: "And do not forget to do good and to share with others, for with such sacrifices God is pleased." We know that serving others is important to God because that's what Jesus did when he lived on earth. He served everyone, both the rich and the poor. He told his followers that when we serve the "least" we are also serving him. These people are not the least important, but rather the forgotten people and those who need help.

The Bible has a lot of other things to say about service. Proverbs 22:9 says, "The generous will themselves be blessed, for they share their food with the poor." When we bless others by giving or serving, God will bless us in return. You might be blessed in some unexpected way, but you will definitely be blessed with the joy that comes from doing the right thing.

Another verse I like is found in Matthew 23:11–12, when Jesus told his followers, "The greatest among you will be your servant. For those who exalt themselves will be humbled, and those who humble themselves will be exalted." To exalt someone means to bring them praise or raise them up. This verse is telling us that the way to receive rewards and recognition is to raise others up by doing things to help and encourage them. We might not always see the rewards or recognition right away. But God sees everything and will remember the things we do to show others his love.

Just like your talents and personality specifically shape your destiny, your interests and gifts can help you find the right places to serve. When you serve in ways that fit well with who you are, you will enjoy the work and make the most impact. Let's talk about some service opportunities that might be a good match for you.

If you are an outgoing people-person (like me!), look for service opportunities that allow you to interact directly with others. You might consider serving food at a soup kitchen or other shelter where you can talk to people and encourage them. You might also consider volunteering to read to inner-city children or helping tutor younger students who are struggling with their schoolwork. As you work to help them, you can develop relationships that will make a difference. You can also look for opportunities for random acts of kindness by complimenting people you run into in your daily life. And it's always great to ask people their names and how you can pray for them!

If you are someone who likes working with your hands, look for ways to serve that use practical skills. Maybe you could help clean up a playground in your neighborhood and fix things that are run down. You could also mow the lawn for an elderly neighbor or get involved with a service group that is tackling a construction project. When you serve with your hands, you will have the satisfaction of seeing the results of your hard work. If you're not a person who likes to be out front, remember that many of the most important things happen behind the scenes; like packing meals for the homeless or helping set up a blood drive. Just find a way to serve that feels comfortable to you!

And finally, use your experiences and unique talents to inspire your service! If you're a singer, go to a nursing home and perform for the residents. If you're a talented artist, see if there is a group home where you could donate your artwork. If you have experience with sports, find a sports camp where you can volunteer.

Even if some of your past experiences aren't positive, you can turn them around and use them for good! If you struggled with a subject in school in the past, find a younger student who is struggling and help them. If you had to walk home by yourself a lot and that felt lonely, find another kid who walks home alone and walk together. You don't have to have the picture-perfect life to offer something. The Bible is filled with examples of people who came from hard circumstances but did what they could—like the poor widow who gave her last coin to the temple, the boy who shared his lunch to feed a hungry crowd, and the single mom who shared the very last thing in her cupboard with a prophet. Whatever you give can be multiplied to infinity in God's hands!

When you serve in these ways, you'll be sure to reap the full benefits of serving others. You'll become an agent of change, if even in the smallest way. Service is good for the mind, body, and soul!

BE A SERVANT

Let's get intentional about serving! Here is a list of some of my favorite organizations to do volunteer work with and why I love them. These are just a few examples of service organizations with good reputations. There are many others, including some right in your own community. Take some time to research different service organizations online with an adult. After you learn more about them, pick your top one. Then talk with an adult about how you can serve in some way with this organization.

Points of Light: I like this organization because they get out into the community and have a hands-on approach.

Ronald McDonald House: This organization is really needed. When you have a sick or injured child in a hospital far from home, these places provide a "home away from home" where the families can stay to be near their child.

Boys & Girls Club: It provides a safe place for kids to go after school. My parents grew up going to Boys & Girls Clubs.

St. Jude Children's Research Hospital: When I
was younger, I used to volunteer answering
the phones for the radiothons to help collect
donations for St. Jude Children's Research
Hospital. This hospital helps children who
are seriously ill at no cost to the families.
Besides treating sick children, they do a lot
of research to help prevent disease. They
rely on donations to support the costs.

FAN Q & A

Q: *Who are your role models?*

A: One of my role models is my mom because she is a great example on how to stay strong and keep faith. Jekalyn Carr is also a great example of living in the spotlight and still glorifying God.

• • • • • • •

Q: *What's the most uncomfortable thing you've ever done out of politeness?*

A: I signed someone's shoe while they were wearing it. It didn't really smell too fresh, but it put the biggest smile on the little boy's face.

Hello, World! Wearing Judy puffs as a baby.

The day we stepped out in faith, leaving Mississippi behind and driving to California, 2012.

I won my first pageant, Little Miss Jackson State University (JSU 2008), along with Hart Jefferson.

Looking sassy for my first dance recital.

My first book drive Jackson, Mississippi, 2014

Our fairy family, Steve, Nathan (not shown), and Allison Kress, celebrating with me on booking K.C. Undercover.

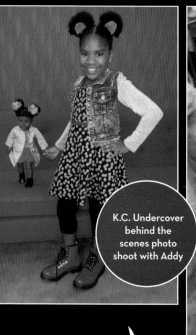

K.C. Undercover behind the scenes photo shoot with Addy

Disneyland fun. Somebody help me!

Making art everywhere I go.

My first Radio Disney Music Awards, 2015

Greeting fans at a personal appearance.

Greeting fans at my first Radio Disney Music Awards.

White House Easter Egg Roll 2016 with the Obamas

Preaching my first sermon, "You Gotta Use What You Got!," 2015. My pastor Michael J. T. Fisher cheers me on.

Leaping into my destiny with First Lady Michelle Obama.

Girl Talk with Serita Jakes and Sarah Jakes-Roberts, Megafest 2017

KCU family posing after our Rio De Janeiro Carnival episode

Styling and profiling in my OWN design.

Rocking my daddy's first design on the red carpet.

My fifth grade graduation at home. LOL!

I LOVE unicorns. My cake was all edible for my double-digit b-day! Thanks Gaspar!

Helping mom overcome her fear of parasailing.

It was cold in the America's Thanksgiving Day parade, Detroit, Michigan.

Enjoying the ocean breeze with my dog, Ginger.

"The Chat" with Priscilla Shirer and Alena Pitts

Star Wars family commercial shoot

Family vacation in Mexico.

Black Girls Rock, 2017, New York

Making music in the studio.

Rocking my own design on the red carpet.

Stokes
Squad, 2018

Robert Cuillard

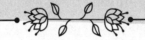

CHAPTER 10

BEHIND THE SCENES

My parents have taught me to keep God first in my life. Everything that I am and everything that I'm doing today is because of God's plan and purpose for my life. Because he has opened doors for me in the entertainment industry, I want to honor him and keep depending on him at all times.

As soon as I open my eyes in the morning, I talk to God. I greet him by saying "Good morning" and thank him for another day. Prayer is extremely important to me and my family. Communication with God keeps me at peace and gives me the strength I need to fulfil my purpose. It's also a time that I can listen for his instruction. I can pray anytime and anywhere because I know God is always with me.

I am in a covenant relationship with God. Covenant is a word that's not used much anymore, but it means an agreement or a promise. So, when I say I'm in a covenant relationship, it means I believe God will always follow through on his promises, and so I need to follow through on my promises too. I need to talk to him and listen when he speaks. You might wonder how God speaks to me. One way God speaks to me is through the Bible. Sometimes when I read the Bible, I feel like the verses I'm reading are the words God wants me to hear. Other times, I just get thoughts or ideas that I know are from him. When I am looking for direction from God or facing a decision, I pray for God to show me what he wants me to understand. My parents do the same. When the ideas we get agree with God's Word, we know that God is speaking to us.

One day I was preparing my sermon for the annual children's day program at my church. I had my notes and message written down, but my dad could see I was a little nervous. Out of nowhere,

Dad asked me what God wanted me to say. I knew God wanted me to give a different message, but I was afraid I wouldn't remember everything and would mess up in front of the congregation. Dad reassured me that because of my covenant with God, he would give me the right words to say from my heart. He was right!

When my parents and I are going through difficult times, or if we are seeking God's direction for something specific, we spend even more time in prayer. In those times, my family may practice fasting—a time when we give up a specific activity, habit, or food—as we wait to learn about God's will. Fasting has nothing to do with diets or weight loss—it has everything to do with drawing closer to God. Sometimes I fast from sweets and focus on listening to God by praying and reading the Bible. You can fast from watching TV, posting on social media, or always being on your phone. It's all about making a sacrifice in your daily routine so you can concentrate on communicating with your Creator. (And if you have questions about fasting, be sure to ask your parents or a church leader.)

I love reading the Bible and have some verses that are very meaningful to me. In Genesis 12:1–3, God tells Abram, "Go from your country, your people and your father's household to the land I will show you. I will make you into a great nation, and I will bless you; I will make your name great, and you will be a blessing. I will bless those who bless you, and whoever curses you I will curse; and all peoples on earth will be blessed through you." These verses meant a lot to me and my family when we made the decision to step out in faith and move to California. We believed God's promise to bless us as we followed him in obedience.

Another verse I love is Philippians 4:13: "I can do all this through him who gives me strength." When I am about to do something that seems too overwhelming for me or makes me afraid, I quote that verse to myself. It always calms my spirit and gives me the confidence I need to move forward.

Our family verse is 1 Corinthians 2:9–10: "What no eye has seen, what no ear has heard, and what no human mind has conceived—the things God has prepared for those who love him—these are the things God has revealed to us by his Spirit." We believe that everything happening to us now, and the things God is going to do in our lives, will be something bigger than we can imagine. It will be something we have not seen or heard before.

When I wonder about the future, a great

reminder for me is found in 2 Corinthians 5:7: "For we live by faith, not by sight." Living by faith means moving forward even though I might not see the road ahead. It means trusting God one step at a time, knowing that he will show me what I need to do when the time is right.

All of these verses are special to me, and the more time I spend reading the Bible, the more I make a conscious effort to keep God first in my life no matter how busy I get. Just like I have to learn scripts, I learn Scripture too. We even read the Bible in the dressing room on set. I want to make sure my focus is always on God and that everything I do is for him. I know that God has blessed me with many amazing opportunities. I understand that my talents and career are gifts from God, and I am in this industry to lead people to Christ.

SO LET'S TALK ABOUT YOU

Maybe you consider yourself an "ordinary" person and wonder if God pays attention to you. Well, just in case you haven't heard it before, I'm here to tell you: GOD LOVES YOU! He loves you just as much as anyone else in the world. And his love never changes. You can't do anything to make him love you more and you also can't do anything to make him love you less. The things that might seem "ordinary" to you can become extraordinary when you live your life for God.

Maybe all of this is new to you and you're a little fuzzy on what it means to know God and have faith in him. As we already discussed, God is your creator. In addition to creating you, God created everything in the world, outer space, and the universe! I love to be in nature because I see proof of God's existence in the mountains, the oceans, trees, and sunset. It helps me remember I'm tiny compared to him. And if he's that big, he really can do anything! If you don't know a lot about God creating the world, I encourage you to read the book of Genesis in the Bible. It explains all the details of how God has always existed and the way he used his power, love, and glory to create the world and fill it with people.

Besides being our creator, the Bible also calls God our Father. We have parents who gave birth to us, but God gave us our existence. Isaiah 64:8 says, "Yet you, LORD, are our Father. We are the clay, you are the potter; we are all the work of your hand."

Maybe the word "father" doesn't leave you with a good feeling inside. Maybe your father isn't in your life, or maybe you have a father who is harsh, unkind, or hurtful in some way. If that's your story, it can be very hard to have a good opinion of God as your father. But it's important to remember that God isn't like our dads. Even if you have a good dad, God is still so much more than a human father. He is entirely perfect; there is nothing bad about him. So, when you see the imperfections of your own dad, know that God doesn't have those flaws. And if you have a wonderful dad in your family, it's incredible to realize that God is an even better father than that!

God is totally trustworthy. He protects, helps, and cares for his children, shows his children right from wrong, and is always with them. We might not always understand everything God does, but because he loves us we don't have to be afraid of him or his plans. He loves us so much he would do anything for us. And the truth is, he already has!

The biggest way God has shown us his love is through Jesus. If you don't know much about Jesus or if you've heard lots of different things about him, let me tell you who I believe Jesus is: Jesus is God's Son. He came to earth and lived as a man while still being fully God. Jesus came for a very special pur-pose: to live a perfect life so he could make things right between us and God. You might be wondering why Jesus had to do that. Did we do something wrong? The short answer is yes.

The Bible says that none of us can live up to God's perfect standards (Romans 3:23). We all do things that go against God's rules for us. That's called sin. Once we sin (even one time), we are separated from God because we are no longer perfect. And we all know that when we do something wrong there is a consequence or punishment. The consequence for sin is being separated from God permanently. But God loves us so much he didn't want that. When Jesus came to earth he never sinned. He did the impossible thing that none of us can do. And after he lived a perfect life, he took our punishment by dying a criminal's death on a cross, even though he didn't deserve it. Because Jesus is God's Son, he came back to life after three days and later went back to heaven.

Believing all of this is what makes Jesus your Savior and makes you a child of God. The Bible says, "For God so loved the world that he gave his one and only Son, that whoever believes in him shall not perish but have eternal life" (John 3:16). So, on top of our punishment being erased, we also get to live with God forever in heaven. And there's also so much we get right now. Knowing Jesus as your Savior means you get to have a meaningful life; everything you do matters. Your life becomes about getting closer to God, sharing his love with everyone around you, and giving him the recognition he deserves. All of that is what it means to grow in your faith.

If you want to know more about God and keep growing in faith, the best thing you can do is read your Bible. Reading the Bible will help you keep learning who God is and how much he loves you. The Bible will show you right from wrong. Doing what's right isn't about being a "good girl" or trying to earn God's love. It's about saying thank you to God for everything he's done. God will help you and give you grace as you learn. If there is only one thing you take away from in this entire book make sure it's this: *God loves you and wants to have a close relationship with you.* It's up to you to decide if you want to have a relationship with him.

Pop Quiz

Pop quiz time! Okay, not really ... this is just for fun! I mentioned some of my favorite Bible verses in this chapter. Here are three of them with some of the words removed. See if you can fill in the blanks! If you need help, you can go back a few pages to reread them, or look them up in a Bible. The version I quote is the NIV (New International Version).

1. For we live by _____, not by _____. (2 Corinthians 5:7)

2. I can do all _____ through _____ who gives me _____. (Philippians 4:13)

3. What no eye has _____, what no ear has _____, and what no human mind has _____—the things _____ has prepared for those who _____ him—these are the things God has revealed to us by his _____. (1 Corinthians 2:9–10)

FAN Q & A

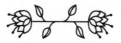

Q: How can you preach at church and still be a kid?

A: Well, I preach because God placed that on the inside of me. It's a part of my purpose. It doesn't interfere at all with me being a kid. Sometimes kids will receive messages better when it is coming from their peers. My preaching also makes adults want to change and live a better life.

• • • • • • •

Q: Where is your favorite place to go for fun?

A: I have a couple of places. I absolutely love Universal Studios! And my all-time favorite place is Disney World! If I could go every week, I would be there. It is so much FUN and full of love and adventure! It makes me dream even more.

CHAPTER 11

BEHIND THE SCENES

God created me to shine so that's what I want to do! I enjoy lighting up a room by creating a positive mood. God gave me a unique purpose for my life and I want to do my best for him. I try to stay positive, follow Christ's example, and never allow anyone to dim my spirit. Jesus, the Son of God, came to be a light to the world. He came to show people how to follow him rather than live in the darkness of the world. I want his light to shine through me, my words, my actions—everything I do.

It isn't easy to stay positive and upbeat all the time—so I have to be intentional about it sometimes. I try to speak positive words and surround myself with positive people. When a negative situation occurs, or I experience rejection or disappointments, I try not to dwell on it for long. I may have to cry it out, but then I am back up and ready to conquer the world.

When I try out for a role and I get a "no" I never let a "no" bring me down. No matter how many I receive, all I need is one YES from God. The opportunities he wants me to have will be mine. If I am not given a role or chosen for something I auditioned for, I know that it wasn't God's plan for me.

By being a positive person, I am also developing a positive reputation. When someone says to me, "I hear you are a joy to work with," I know it's because I try to treat everyone the way I want to be treated. A kind word and a loving heart can go a long way and leave a good impression. Sometimes my mom and I make cupcakes, chocolate-covered strawberries, or our famous Rice Krispy treats and bring them to the set for the crew. We put them in a cute bag and attach a Bible verse. It's our way of putting smiles on their faces and making the day a little brighter. It's often the little things we do that can turn someone's day around.

I believe that showing love and kindness to others is one of the best ways to let my light shine for Jesus. Every person has value and deserves to be treated with respect. I try to find the good in others, just like I hope people see the good in me. I have a friend who I met in an acting class who is a super nice guy, but he is often bullied and teased. We don't live in the same state, so one year, I surprised him and showed up at his birthday party. I was so glad I could go. I wanted him to know that he's important to me. Another time, my family took him to Disney World and we had a blast! I care about others because that's what Jesus does.

I appreciate the opportunities I have had to preach the gospel to an audience, but my life has to speak the same message. Actions speak louder than words, and people will not listen to what I say if my life doesn't line up with my words. I know that people are watching me because I have times when I am in the spotlight. If people are watching me, then I want them to see that I am a positive and loving person who loves the Lord. My prayer is that others will be drawn to Jesus by my example. I often thank God on social media, or offer fun Bible trivia games. I've even posted invitations for my work friends to join me for church. Some people seem surprised that I am on a TV show and talk so freely about God in public. Others thank me for sharing my faith because they want to have that faith too.

Sticking to my beliefs and standing up for what is right can be hard. My parents help me decide which events or concerts are okay to attend, and which ones are not. I also know I need to be strong when it comes to roles I might be offered. One time someone asked me if I would ever consider accepting a role that included cursing. I replied, "No—not at all! I can't compromise my beliefs for money or fame." One of the producers overheard the conversation and thought that was crazy. But later, that same producer told me how much she enjoyed working with me. Then she added, "Trinitee, you keep believing and holding true to what's in your heart and don't ever change—you will go a long way!" I hugged her and was thankful that she saw something special in my life. She had a change of heart, and I know God did that! I just want to keep shining the light wherever I am.

SO LET'S TALK ABOUT YOU

You have a light to shine too, and I pray you let your light shine brightly and keep other people from snuffing it out. At times it can be hard to live by what you believe in. The world throws all kinds of stuff at us and pop culture tries to tell us who we're supposed to be. I've learned to tune out all that noise. I focus on the voices that truly matter—my parents, good friends, people I trust, and God. I let those messages guide me. And that's my advice to you: don't listen to the pressures society puts on you. Don't let magazines or social media tell you what you need to look like or how you need to act. Know who you are and what you love, and listen to the people who support you. The funny thing about pop culture is that things are always changing. So even if you try to be what pop culture tells you to be, or look like what they say is beautiful, in a couple of months it will all change. Chasing after that kind of life is exhausting. God wants you to be free from living up to others' expectations. When you know he loves and approves of you, you can let go of trying to keep up and just be who you are.

It's important to actively find ways to live a positive life. Having good things to give your energy to helps you focus on what matters and not be influenced by all the things that can drag you down. One way to do that is to get involved in positive activities. Find activities that allow you to pursue your passions in healthy ways and give you purpose. Maybe it's dance classes, art classes, sports, student government, volunteer work, music, or an after-school club. When you have good things to fill your schedule, you don't have time for things that aren't positive. I let my talents and passions drive my commitments and shape my schedule. It's allowed me to spend my time doing things that make me happy and determined. And being involved in those kinds of things makes it easy to shine my light because I feel energized and in tune with my Creator. When you're busy with things that make you feel alive and give you meaning, unhelpful activities and influences just don't seem appealing.

In the same way you should look for good things to build you up, you want to actively avoid activities and events that could pull you down. It's important to protect yourself and be on guard against things that could be a negative influence on your life. Anything that could harm your mind, body, commitment to your beliefs, or break your parents' rules is a negative influence. Things that could hurt other people physically or emotionally are also negative activities to avoid. You can shine your light in the ways you handle invitations or temptations to participate in negative things. For example, if a group of kids at school tries to get you to do something that is wrong, you can say "no" confidently and kindly. It's possible to be strong and nice at the same time. You don't have to put others down when you don't agree with their decisions. You can even invite them to participate in something more positive to turn the situation around. Knowing what you believe and why will help you stand strong and stay away from things that aren't good. It can be helpful to have a plan for how to handle negative situations, like who you should call if you suddenly find yourself in a bad spot or what you plan to say when you want to avoid certain events.

A big part of staying away from the wrong activities is staying away from peers who may have a negative influence on you. Staying away from them doesn't mean being rude or ugly; it just means not allowing them into the inner part of your life. The Bible says, "Bad company corrupts good character" (1 Corinthians 15:33). That's why it's so important to hang around people who build you up, and you can build them up in return. You can always encourage your peers by your example. Sometimes they will notice there is something different about you, even from a distance, and that might encourage them to change. Be willing to lift others up with a positive example, kind words, or a smile. But don't spend the majority of your time with people who make you feel yucky or whose actions cause you to compromise your standards. When you choose your friends wisely, you'll maintain a valuable reputation and protect yourself from danger and getting off track from your goals.

Letting your light shine and living for God all come down to standing up for what is right. It's about what you purposely do and don't do. It's about loving others and sticking up for them, even when it's not the cool thing to do. It's about being the one to stop gossip, bullying, and hatefulness, even if you're the only one speaking up. It's about not being ashamed to make right choices and follow the rules, even if it's not popular. When you live for God, you can have the confidence that no other opinion matters. When you choose to go against the messages of the world, his love and light will shine in all that you do.

Be Bold

I know it can be hard to speak up about your belief in God. I encourage you to speak up as much as possible. Sometimes silence sends the opposite message of your beliefs. Here are some tips that have helped me be bold in sharing my love for God with others:

1. Live a godly life by example. Let your actions speak louder than your words.
2. Keep having conversations about God. The more you do, the more it will build your confidence in sharing your beliefs.
3. Have a movie night with your friends and watch a Christian movie that helps them understand more about God.
4. Do mission work with your friends so they can see your faith in action.
5. Start a game of Bible trivia on social media. It helps open conversations about your beliefs.
6. Tell your testimony—your personal story of what God has done for you and your love for him.
7. Stay passionate about your beliefs and your love for God. Keep reading the Bible, listening to music that helps you worship God, and keep learning through sermons, books, and Bible studies.

FAN Q & A

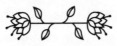

Q: *Do you like the paparazzi or do you like your privacy?*

A: I like having the paparazzi around but sometimes anonymity would be great while eating at a restaurant or trying to run to the mall really quick.

• • • • • • •

Q: *What's your biggest fear?*

A: My biggest fear is that I'll get bitten by a snake or a spider. They really freak me out.

CHAPTER 12

Just Be You

BEHIND THE SCENES

Every so often my dad asks me, "Trinitee, who are you?" I know the answer to that question, and I know he asks me that to remind me to stay true to who I am. I am Trinitee—a child of God, chosen for a specific purpose. I am Trinitee—with unique gifts, talents, and opportunities to show others what it means to trust in God and follow Jesus.

I want people to look at my life and want a life of faith like I have. I want them to believe that all things are possible and that the sky is not the limit—to go after what's beyond the sky and the clouds to what you can't even see! There are no limits with God. I pray every day that God will allow my life to be an example so others can see what faith in God looks like. Even though I may never meet them in person, millions of people are watching me. I want to impact the world in a positive way. I don't want my story to just be about big dreams, but about big faith.

I am young, but I can still be a role model to other girls. And that's what I want to do. I have good role models in my life and there are many women whom I admire. I'd love to tell you about some of them, so I'll start with my mom. I admire her because she has overcome many obstacles in her life, and never allowed them to stop her from achieving her dreams. She overcame sexual abuse and a negative childhood environment. She was the first person on her mom's side of the family to earn a college degree and then an MBA. She was an inspiration to her family and now others have gone on to earn degrees. She is a published author and told me that someday I would be an author too. She motivates others to strive for greatness and she is hilarious (that's where I get my personality). The most important thing is that she is a praying woman, and that is the example I want to follow.

I also admire Oprah Winfrey for being a strong woman, overcoming many challenges, and being a world changer. When Oprah speaks, people listen. It seems that everything she does turns to gold. She is very generous and is a blessing to many people. The Bible reminds us that being generous is important. Deuteronomy 15:10 says, "Give generously to them and do so without a grudging heart; then because of this the LORD your God will bless you in all your work and in everything you put your hand to." The other thing I love about Oprah is that we are both from Mississippi, and I often joke that Mississippi girls change the world.

Yara Shahidi is another person whom I admire. She is a young adult activist who is using her voice to make a change. I hope to be in the political arena someday, and she is leading the way for me in her humble, yet powerful way. She is also dedicated to education and makes that a high priority in her philanthropic work.

Of course, I admire Michelle Obama—our first African American First Lady of the United States of America! What's not to love? Her leadership, intelligence, and strong character inspire me. She has a glowing personality, she is highly intelligent, and is a powerful speaker. She also showed me how to be graceful under pressure.

Last, but not least, is Zendaya. If she wanted to wear orange hair on the red carpet, she would wear it with such confidence that you wouldn't even think about it being orange. She does what she feels is right and she owns it. Zendaya believes in herself and I love that about her.

I admire these women not because of where they started, but because of what they stand for. They confidently stand for hope and change, and they are not afraid to just be who they are. I want to follow their examples. I am a leader and march to my own beat. I want to encourage other girls to do the same.

SO LET'S TALK ABOUT YOU

Having the courage to be yourself comes from having healthy self-confidence. It can take time to build your confidence, so be patient with yourself as you grow into your own self-esteem. To build self-confidence you need to talk to yourself in a positive way and stop filling your mind with negative thoughts about who you are. It's also important to never talk badly about yourself. Talking badly about yourself is not humility—it's putting down one of God's unique and wonderful creations!

Self-confidence is knowing what your talents, gifts, and strengths are and owning them. You recognize they are gifts God has given you. The purpose of his gifts is to fill your life with meaning, to share his love with others, and to honor him. Since each person is made uniquely by God, we all have our own specific destiny to fill. That means we don't have to compare ourselves to others or be worried that we'll miss out on our purpose in life. When you believe that God is directing your life and leading you into the plans he has for you, it can give you security that you will be all that he wants you to be and do all that he wants you to do.

Even when you know your destiny is safe in God's hands, it's still normal to be fearful about chasing your dreams and what others think. The important thing is to not allow fear to control your actions and your life. Fear is not part of God's path for us. The Bible says, "For the Spirit God gave us does not make us timid, but gives us power, love, and self-discipline" (2 Timothy 1:7). If fear keeps sneaking up on you and trying to steal your joy and confidence, you can silence its power by moving in faith. That means you do the big things you are afraid to do, and you don't listen to the negative voices. You don't have to fear failure. As long as you are trying and chasing your dreams, failure doesn't exist. Even when things don't go the way you hope, you are still learning, growing, and moving forward on your path. The only way you can fail is if you don't try. When you give up you hold yourself back from becoming everything you can be.

Another way to silence fear when it's coming on strong is to repeat your goals and truths about yourself daily. Like we've talked about before, it can be helpful to say it out loud in front of a mirror. When you're filling your ears with positivity and truth, it drowns out the lies and uncertainty of fear. You can even ask your friends and family what positive things they see in you and begin to collect those truths too. You don't have to sit back and be a victim of fear. You can fight it as a brave warrior and not let it hold you back from all that is waiting for you. Bravery will grow your confidence and help you become comfortable with who you are. Confidence is a very attractive quality and it helps others be comfortable around you too.

Living with a brave, confident mindset can make it easier to support the girls around you. And when you give them respect, it encourages them to respect you in return. Supporting others and lifting others up means encouraging them and not having an attitude of jealousy. We all have different gifts to use in this world, and we all have a specific mission in life.

One way I like to support the girls around me is to cheer them on. I let them know they are doing a great job, no matter what it is. I try to attend other girls' events and parties to let them know I support what they are doing and how proud of them I am. I love to encourage people I meet in person and my supporters online. My message to them is to dream BIG and expect to see their dreams come true, and, most importantly, to NEVER GIVE UP!

I hope that the life of faith I live encourages you to experience that type of faith in your own life. One of my biggest desires is for you to know that if you believe, ALL things are possible. It doesn't matter what circumstances, trials, or challenges you may face. Work hard, have integrity, and be true to yourself. Don't try to be like anyone else. There is no one else in this world exactly like you, so just be you!

THAT'S INSPIRING!

Here's some inspirational advice I've collected from different women over the years. Some of it comes from famous women, and some from women I've known in my personal life. I hope these gems of wisdom encourage you to be the best you!

1. Never dummy yourself down or dim your light to make someone else more comfortable.
2. Always use the voice that you have been given.
3. Use the platform God gives you for his glory.
4. Give a girl the right pair of shoes, and she will conquer the world. (Marilyn Monroe said this to show how if you start with the right foundation, you can do great things. And I love having the right pair of shoes.)
5. Always keep God first in every area of your life. That is his rightful position.
6. Never stop praying.
7. Don't try to be like someone else; God wants to bless the true you.
8. Always have integrity and keep your word.
9. Be nice to everyone no matter what walk of life they come from.
10. If you need help, ask for it.

FAN Q & A

Q: If you could work with any famous producer, director, or actor, who would it be and why?

A: I want to work with Steven Spielberg because well . . . he's STEVEN SPIELBERG. LOL. He has such a special gift. I am also looking forward to working with Oprah, Tyler Perry, and Devon Franklin.

• • • • • • •

Q: If you weren't acting, what would you want to do?

A: I would want to be a private investigator. One of my favorite shows is *Murder She Wrote*. I love how Angela Lansbury plays an investigator and solves the crimes. In my downtime I would be a pastry chef. I love to bake and create designs with icing and fondant.

Q: Do you have just as much sass as Judy?

A: I have a good amount of sass but I know how to control it. My parents won't allow me to be so smart-mouthed, but the character of Judy didn't care. I loved playing Judy.

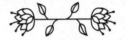

CHAPTER 13

Body, Mind, and Soul

You've read the previous chapters and I hope you've enjoyed them, but we're not quite finished! I've created a bonus chapter—it's like three chapters in one. I want to spend some time talking about how you can take care of yourself because you are worth it! It's more than just getting a good night's sleep or doing your homework. It's about taking care of your WHOLE self—inside and out. God created you with a body, mind, and soul. Together they define who you are. That's why it's important to take care of yourself, from the hair on your head to the toes on your feet and everything in between.

If you're a kid or teenager, now is a great time to start healthy habits that can be a part of the rest of your life. Taking care of your whole self means paying attention to what you personally need in every area. You need to pay a lot of attention to how you're feeling inside and out so you can be aware when things are out of balance. When you aren't feeling your best in a certain area, make some changes so you can get back to a good place. Let's take a look at some ways you can care for the three parts of your being!

EVERY BODY IS BEAUTIFUL: BEHIND THE SCENES

Your body is the part of you that everyone sees, and bodies come in all different shapes and sizes! I want to understand my body type because it helps when choosing the right clothes. Just because a certain style might be cute or trendy, doesn't mean it's the right look for me, so I try to find clothes that work well with my body type. My body type might be different from some of my friends, but I accept my body the way that it is. When I look in the mirror, I have positive thoughts about the body God has given me. Having a beautiful body is not about being a certain size, it's about loving the body you have because every *body* is beautiful.

Besides accepting my body, I know it's important to take care of it, and there are many ways I try to do that. One way is to eat a healthy, well-balanced diet. I am originally from the south, and I love fried chicken and buttery cornbread! I know that kind of food is not so healthy, so I try to eat better kinds of food as well. Changing my eating habits has been an on-going process, but I know it's important and I'm glad that I am doing it. I don't deprive myself of some of the food I love, I just eat it in moderation and make sure most of my meals and snacks are good for me. Some of my favorite healthy foods are a veggie hash that my daddy created, avocado egg rolls, quiche, and a panko-crusted homemade tempeh burger. My favorite in-between-meal snacks are carrots with hummus, kale chips dipped in ranch dressing, granola cups made with Greek yogurt and fresh berries, and white cheddar popcorn—yum!

I know that getting enough exercise is also important if I want to have a healthy body, but this is challenging for me when I have to be at the studio almost every day. What has really helped is exercising to YouTube videos at home. That way I can fit workouts into my schedule without it being too time consuming. When I have a break in my schedule, I have a personal trainer and do CrossFit training, which includes a variety of exercises to build my strength and endurance. I really didn't like working out at first, but knew I needed to do it to be strong and healthy. Now I love going to CrossFit because I love the challenge!

Just as eating healthy food and getting regular exercise is important, getting enough rest is important. To be honest, if my mom didn't make me rest, I would probably keep going, going, going. I remember one time that I was so busy, my body just crashed. I went to sit on my bed to read a book, and I fell asleep and slept for hours! I know that taking naps is not common with kids my age, but I still need them. Sometimes it's only for thirty minutes during lunch when I am at the studio, but if I am at home, I might take a nap for an hour. I also have a pretty early bedtime compared to most kids I know, but that's what works for me. Getting a good night's sleep gives me energy for the next day. Unless I have an event or a late day on the set, I am in bed by 7:30 or 8:00. I usually get up at 5:45, so my day starts very early. When I am on a break from work or it's the weekend, I get to sleep in later.

My body is the body that God gave me, and I want to honor him by taking good care of it. Besides doing things that are good for my body, I also don't want to do things that are bad for me. Smoking cigarettes leads to lung disease. Using drugs and alcohol can lead to other serious diseases. These things are not only harmful to my body, they can also destroy my life. With God's help, I will choose to keep my body free of anything that can harm it. I've only got one body, and I want it to be beautiful.

SO LET'S TALK ABOUT YOU

What are your thoughts when it comes to taking care of your body? Are you someone who loves playing sports and being active? Is it hard for you to want to eat healthy because junk food tastes so good? It doesn't matter if being healthy comes naturally to you; there are things everyone can do to take good care of their bodies.

The most important way to take care of your body is to think about it in a positive way. You have to be confident with your body and accept it the way it is. God made your body to do amazing things and he sees it as a wonderful work of creation. That's why it's so important to take care of ourselves—it's a way we can honor God because he made us. It can be easy to compare your size and looks to others. The media sends us messages about how we need to look all the time. But trying to make yourself look the way society tells you to look doesn't mean you are taking good care of your body. Loving yourself is taking good care of your body and that means eating healthy, staying active, sleeping enough, and taking care of your unique physical needs.

I've shared with you some of the ways I try to eat healthy and what has worked for me. Eating a healthy diet can mean a lot of different things depending on your needs, body type, preferences, and values. It's good to talk to an adult with knowledge about nutrition to help you figure out what's best for you. A lot of people have food allergies that affect what they can eat. If you have food allergies, you need to keep that in mind when thinking about your healthy eating habits. Some people prefer high protein diets and others choose to be vegetarians because that's best for them. What matters is that you have a balanced diet that gives you the right proportion of vitamins, nutrients, protein, fats, and carbohydrates. That might sound like a lot of science information, but there are plenty of websites you can research with an adult to understand what all of that means. No matter what path you choose for your eating habits, remember it's never a good idea to stop eating to try to lose weight or to do anything to make you get rid of what you've already eaten. The best thing to keep in mind is that food is your fuel; it's what helps you live and move and do the things you love. So, when you're making choices about what to eat and how to craft your meals, think about putting helpful, good fuel into your body. That kind of food will help you to be your best!

Some other healthy habits to develop are getting enough sleep, keeping yourself clean, and staying physically active. You know a little bit about my sleep habits and what is best for me and my schedule. What about you? Depending on your age, you probably need about nine or ten hours of sleep a night. If you're not getting enough sleep regularly, start thinking about ways you can change that. Maybe a new bedtime routine can help or maybe you need to start going to bed earlier. It can be hard if you're a night owl and you get up early for school, but if you make it a habit, chances are your body will adjust. Keep technology out of your room at night so you're not distracted and your mind isn't fuzzy from the screens. Make sure you're comfortable when you go to bed and that you're ready for the next day. And it always helps to say your bedtime prayers!

Making sure that you're fresh and clean is extremely important when taking care of yourself. We should make sure that we brush our teeth, wash our face, and comb our hair. Taking regular baths and showers is important for your health and helps you smell good too! If personal hygiene feels like a chore to you, try to think of ways to make it fun. Maybe you can put on a concert in the shower or watch a funny YouTube video while you brush your teeth. When your body feels good, you feel good about your body.

When it comes to exercise, there's no limit to the fun ways you can stay fit! If you're an athlete, exercising is built into your practices and games. You get to have fun while strengthening your body. If you don't play sports or don't enjoy doing physical activities, see if you can find creative ways to get moving. Maybe you can go on a walk with a friend and have good conversations. If you live near the mountains, take a hike and think of it as a way to enjoy the beauty of God's creation. You can try swimming, dance classes, going to a trampoline park, or riding your bike. Just find something you enjoy that gets your body in motion. A good habit is to limit your screen time to an hour or two a day, or not watch TV or play video games until you've had some exercise. But remember to keep it all in balance. It only takes a little regular exercise each day to stay healthy.

No matter how well you eat, exercise, or sleep, some kids have health issues that affect their everyday lives. I love being outdoors and enjoying the smell of fresh air and the sights and sounds of nature. But I have an allergy called cholinergic urticaria that keeps me inside when the days are too hot. It means that I am allergic to my own body heat, so I just can't get too hot either outdoors or indoors. It can be hard at times, but I know God is helping me live a healthy life despite this rare allergy, and I am looking forward to when God heals me. If you have physical challenges, just do the best you can to be as healthy as you can be. Maybe you can't eat carrots with hummus, or do CrossFit. Maybe you need more or less sleep than I do. That's okay! You can ask a parent or another grownup you trust to help you find what works for you so you can have a strong and healthy body that you love. God knows your physical limitations and he will help you. Keep praying for healing and a positive perspective, just like I do.

Taking care of your physical self all comes down to respecting your body. Treat it as a valuable, priceless treasure. First Corinthians 6:19–20 says: "Do you not know that your bodies are temples of the Holy Spirit, who is in you, whom you have received from God? You are not your own; you were bought at a price. Therefore, honor God with your bodies."

Learn to love yourself exactly the way God made you and embrace everything about your body that's unique. We only get one body in this life, so let's be kind to ourselves!

DADDY'S DELICIOUS VEGGIE HASH RECIPE

Choose any veggies that you like—onions, bell peppers, potatoes, corn, mushrooms, broccoli, cauliflower—and chop them up into small pieces.

In a nonstick pan or wok, sauté the veggies in peanut oil until they are tender. Add lemon pepper, peppercorn, and Italian seasoning. You can also add some veggie meat crumble if you want. Then add some sweet chili sauce. Stir for a few more minutes. Serve and enjoy!

PROTECTING THE POWER OF YOUR MIND: BEHIND THE SCENES

Your mind is what allows you to think, learn, and remember. Education is a critical part of your growing-up years because that is how we accumulate knowledge. Because of my career in television, I don't go to school like most other kids my age. While I am on set I have a studio teacher who makes sure I get the necessary hours of instruction to meet the state's educational requirements. We have a curriculum that the teacher uses, and my mom also uses some homeschool materials to make sure I stay ahead of my grade level. I often complete academic workbooks when I'm in the car. It's easy for kids to fall behind in school when they work five days a week, but my mom is determined to not let that happen to me. My parents want my education to come before acting.

Learning new things is something I really enjoy. I would like to attend Harvard University or London Business School after I graduate from high school. I am not sure how all that is going to happen since I also have goals for my acting career, but I will do it even if it means taking classes online. My mom was the first one from her mom's side of the family

171

to earn a college degree. I want to keep that legacy going.

I believe education is important because learning is a way to gain knowledge, and knowledge is power. Some students learn quickly, while others may have to work harder on certain subjects. It's okay if you don't get all As, and if you don't, it doesn't mean you are not smart. The important thing is to do the best you can and keep learning. It's also okay to ask for help. There are some very good tutors who can help you study and understand your subjects better.

Besides academic learning, it's important to fill your mind with good things. I do that by reading the Bible or listening to worship music. When I was younger, I loved watching VeggieTales episodes. I still watch them when I can because they teach good lessons. I try hard to keep my mind focused on positive thoughts and am careful about what I allow in my brain. I don't want to tarnish my head with inappropriate movies, books, or TV shows. These things can give me impure thoughts, which I don't want to have.

Gaining knowledge and keeping my mind fixed on good things are ways that I can have a healthy mind, but I also want to gain wisdom. Knowledge is something that we learn, and wisdom is applying knowledge to everyday life. James 1:5 says, "If any of you lacks wisdom, you should ask God, who gives generously to all without finding fault, and it will be given to you." I love this verse because it tells me that if I want wisdom, all I need to do is ask the Lord and he will give it to me!

I want to keep learning and filling my mind with things that will help me achieve my goals and live the life God has for me. It's not easy, but with the help of my parents and lots of prayer, I know I can do it!

SO LET'S TALK ABOUT YOU

Have you ever wondered *what's the big deal with learning, anyway?* A lot of education has to do with preparing for your future and developing your academic smarts so you can pursue your career. But there is a lot more to learning than that. Learning helps you gain skills to use in all areas of your life. It keeps you in touch with the world around you and helps you relate to different people and cultures. Increasing your knowledge keeps your mind fresh and exercises your brain muscles like working out does for the rest of your muscles.

As you realize that learning is an important part of your life and well-being, it can give you motivation to do your best in school. Doing your best means you are working hard and performing to the best of your ability. You try to learn as much as you can from each class and experience. You don't have to compare yourself or be in competition with others. You see how learning opportunities can help you with your goals and make you a well-rounded person. And doing well in school will help give you the best options for pursuing your career goals in the future.

You might not know exactly what you want to do for your career, but even if it's not totally clear, you can still think about how to use education to shape your future. Maybe going to college is a good choice for you, so you can have a broad education and find your area of passion. Maybe a technical school is a good fit for you if there is a special skill you want to devote your time to. You can think about getting involved in a family business, going to art school, or training under an expert in a certain field. If you need help narrowing your focus, school counselors can help you. Once you have an idea of the direction you want to go, you can start planning your education around that goal. And if you change your mind later, remember that no learning is ever wasted!

Besides keeping your mind sharp with academics, it's important to fill your mind with good things. Have you ever noticed how what you think about affects your mood? Like how you feel down after watching a sad movie or when you get happy as you picture your dreams coming true. Our minds are powerful and have a huge influence on the way we see ourselves and our lives. That's why it's necessary to keep positive thoughts in your head and develop healthy ways of thinking. Music with upbeat and positive messages keeps your mind in a good place. That way when a song gets stuck in your head, good things are repeating over and over. I've mentioned before how I use positive self-talk to affirm myself every day. The more you say something, the more you believe it. If we have that power, let's choose to believe good things about ourselves! It's also helpful to keep Bible verses around you to fill your mind with God's truth. A good verse to remember is Philippians 4:8: "Whatever is true, whatever is noble, whatever is right, whatever is pure, whatever is lovely, whatever is admirable—if anything is excellent or praiseworthy—think about such things."

When negative, scary, or unhealthy thoughts

creep into my mind, I don't dwell on them. Sometimes I imagine the thought being caught up inside a bubble and the bubble floating out of my head, far away from me. That visual really helps me separate myself from bad thoughts. And if I'm ever having a hard time letting go of negative thoughts I talk to my mom and dad or another adult I trust. I try to avoid dark, violent, or disturbing movies and music because I know those things won't bring anything good into my mind. I also protect my mind from thoughts that are inappropriate by praying. I know that what I *don't* put into my mind is just as important as what I do.

As you develop good mental habits, you'll gain wisdom too. Wisdom uses your knowledge in the best way possible to make good choices. Wisdom is a topic the Bible talks about a lot. Proverbs 4:7 (NLT) says, "Getting wisdom is the wisest thing you can do! And whatever else you do, develop good judgment." Wisdom might sound like something that only older people have, but it's possible to have it as a kid. Wisdom is understanding what you can control, accepting what you can't, and making the best choices possible. It also depends on God's grace, because it's impossible to do everything right 100 percent of the time. As you grow in your knowledge and experience of the world, ask yourself how you can use all of it to be a better person and do the right thing.

Mostly, I hope you remember your mind is one of the most powerful tools you have. It can be hard to stay motivated in school, but remember how much you have to gain by studying and developing your mind. Find creative ways to exercise your brain and always be willing to talk about new topics with people around you. There's no limit to how far your mind can take you!

STRAIN THAT BRAIN

Just like our bodies need exercise, our brains need exercise too. Doing jigsaw puzzles and crossword puzzles, or playing games like Scrabble, Sudoku, or Letter Mix are good activities for your brain. These games and activities are not only fun, but they help to stimulate your brain.

LOVE YOUR SOUL, SISTER!
BEHIND THE SCENES

Your soul is the part of you that is not physical; it is the part that lasts forever. There is something down inside us that is beyond the explanation of science. The Bible calls it our soul or spirit. I care for my soul by spending time reading the Bible every day. Some people refer to the Bible as God's Word. With so much technology available to us today, it's easy to read the Bible every day. You can use Bible apps, audio Bibles, and you can even get Bible verses emailed to you. I might not have a lot of time to study God's Word each day, but I always start my mornings by reading something from the Bible. I believe it helps keep my focus where it needs to be, and it helps me keep my priorities in order.

My life can be challenging and even difficult at times. Sometimes I am just busy and overwhelmed. It's during those times that I wonder if God hears me or if he is still with me. Whenever I feel that spiritual disconnect, I claim what I know to be true. Joshua 1:9 says, "Be strong and courageous. Do not be afraid; do not be discouraged, for the LORD your God will be with you wherever you go." Even though I may have moments when I don't *feel* like

God is with me, I *know* that he is with me and that I am never alone. I need to remember that God is always near me, and if I speak to him in prayer or spend time in the Word, I will feel close to him again. I love the words in Psalm 145:18: "The LORD is near to all who call on him, to all who call on him in truth."

Besides my personal time with God, we spend time with the Lord together as a family. We study the Bible together to help us grow spiritually and stay connected to God. My parents also have what we call "A Family Shut In." It's something our church in Mississippi used to do when we lived there, but now we do it in our home. We turn off our phones and TV and only communicate with God and each other. I tease my parents by telling them it's "old school," but I know it's a great way to focus on God without all the distractions and interruptions. We also attend church services every week, unless we are out of town. Another thing we like to do is sing worship songs together. Most of the time we are way out of tune, but the Bible says to make a joyful noise to the Lord and that is what we do!

When we continue to fill our souls with truth and promises from God's Word, what happens on the inside will show on the outside. God's love will flow through us as we interact with people. A smile, a hug, or a kind word will communicate to others that we have a kind and loving spirit. My parents have always taught me to be someone who treats others with love and respect—and that's how I want to be known.

> "What good will it be for someone to gain the whole world, yet forfeit their soul? Or what can anyone give in exchange for their soul?"
>
> (Matthew 16:26)

SO LET'S TALK ABOUT YOU

Depending on your background, you might not have thought much about your soul. You might not really understand what your soul is. It can be hard to understand things that are more abstract, but here are some thoughts to get you started. To God, your soul is the most important thing about you. He cares more about the souls of people than anything else in the world. In fact, God thinks your soul is worth so much he sent his Son, Jesus, to die on the cross so your soul could be saved.

Taking care of your soul can be harder than

taking care of your body and mind. You have to really dig deep into who you are, where you have strengths and difficulties, and connect with God in a personal way. But there are practical, real ways you can take care of your soul and protect the most important part of who you are. Even if you haven't grown up going to church, you can still do lots of things to grow your spiritual self.

Because your soul is the part of you that allows you to have a relationship with God, your relationship with him is the place to start. When you begin connecting with God on a regular basis, you will start to understand more about your soul and how you keep it healthy. As we've already talked about, the best ways to connect with God are through reading the Bible and praying. Reading the Bible is how God talks to your soul. It helps you see the things in your soul that you need to work on, like bad habits or ways you aren't living how God wants you to. The Bible also empowers your soul as you fill yourself with the truth about who God is and what it means to be a part of his family.

Prayer is how your soul talks to God. It allows you to tell God your needs, fears, desires, and ask him for help. Praying helps you focus on the things God wants you to focus on and connects your soul to him no matter where you are or what you're doing. It helps you press pause on the world around you and re-center yourself. Sometimes it can be hard to be still and quiet and talk to God. But just keep doing it even if it feels weird. God already knows what you're thinking and feeling, so just tell him what's in your heart. When you open up to God about the deep things in your life, you will discover more about your soul and your spiritual needs.

Taking care of your soul also means you do things God's way. God knows what's best for the deepest part of your being, and doing things his way will strengthen your soul. Sometimes that looks like stepping away from unhealthy friendships when others don't treat you with kindness. Other times it looks like doing the right thing even if it seems uncool. It can be hard to do what's right. But you know that good feeling you get inside when you've done the right thing? That's your soul being filled up!

The final part of taking care of your soul is protecting it. Just like you don't want to put a bunch of junk in your mind or body, you don't want to put bad things in your soul. For me that means staying away from evil or dark things. I don't like to give time or attention to things that go against God's word;

things like violence, gossip, talking about scary or creepy things, or watching movies about evil spirits. Those things can really affect you inside, whether you realize it or not. The best thing you can do is think of your soul as your most treasured possession. Do everything you can to guard it, as if it's worth a hundred-million dollars!

Even if it's new for you to talk about your soul, I hope you realize just how important it is. Taking care of the inmost part of yourself will have a big impact on the way you feel physically and mentally. When your soul is right, everything else becomes clearer. Never forget how much God loves you and wants to be a part of your life. Remember that you're more valuable than diamonds and every part of you is worth caring for.

A POEM FOR MY SOUL SISTERS

Everyone has a soul.

It's part of you that makes you whole.

Protect your soul and be aware,

the devil is real—he's everywhere.

Keep God first in your heart.

If you want wisdom, that's where you start.

The more you learn, and the more you grow

your life will shine with a joyful glow.

Don't be afraid when you're under attack.

Jesus will help you to fight back.

Jesus died for you and me,

To save our souls and set us free.

His love is better than silver or gold.

I am a free soul,

I am BLESSED and I am BOLD.

FAN Q & A

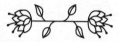

Q: What is one thing all young girls should know in order to be the best version of themselves?

A: Girls should know that God loves them exactly the way he made them. They should never change anything about themselves to please people.

• • • • • • •

Q: Where is your dream vacation?

A: I want to take a two-month vacation and travel to Paris, Italy, Rome, London, and then to Africa! That is going to be the time of my life when I do it. I will be sure to record a video diary so that you can travel with me!

CHAPTER 14

Trinitee and Beyond

BEHIND THE SCENES

The fact that you're reading this book is an answer
to prayer. Becoming an author was on my list of
goals—it was something I had envisioned and
wanted to achieve. Only God could have made
this happen. I trusted him to open the doors for me
in publishing and he has. So, what's next for me?
Changing the world is next! I have many goals, projects, and dreams, and I'm moving forward one step
at a time.

As I shared in Chapter 2, I would love to have

my own TV show, book some action-packed films, and perform on Broadway. I also want to write, direct, and produce movies and TV shows. Some of the people I admire in the entertainment world are Oprah, Tyler Perry, Steven Spielberg, Robert Downey Jr., Denzel Washington, Viola Davis, The Rock, and Morgan Freeman. It would be a dream come true to work with any of them someday.

I plan to keep singing and being involved in music. I want my songs and music to be timeless and played for generations to come. My goal in music is to take listeners on a journey that will last a lifetime, just like my favorite singers—Adele, Beyoncé, Meghan Trainor, Michael Jackson, Janet Jackson, and Luke Bryan. Someday I hope to join the ranks of those who have received an Emmy, Grammy, Oscar, and Tony (EGOT), like Whoopi Goldberg. I will be a megastar. It's a lofty goal, but if God wants me to accomplish it, he will help me.

I enjoy traveling and want to visit all seven continents by the time I am sixteen. I can't wait to visit Africa! I'd love to do some mission work there and go on an African safari.

As I look ahead to the future, Habakkuk 2:2 (NKJV) really speaks to me: "write the vision and make it plain." That's what it's all about for me! I write down the ideas, dreams, and goals that I have. If these are from God, then I need to be serious about following through. Writing down my vision in plain and simple language allows me to focus on what I believe God is leading me to do. But as I pursue my goals and dreams, I want to stand for what is right and share my faith, hope, and joy with the world. I'll stand for something great, even if it costs me everything. I want to leave behind a legacy of faith—that's what's most important.

When people think of me or hear my name, I hope it motivates them to not only have faith, but to activate it by pursuing every dream that is deep down inside of them. Faith in God is what enables me to walk in my destiny. It's because of faith that I will be able to live a life that will change the world for good.

Oh yeah—and here's one more thing that's on my list—I want to go skydiving!

SO LET'S TALK ABOUT YOU

Right now is a great time for you to think about your future. I know you have dreams and talents inside of you and it's time to let them out! What do you want to achieve in five years? Ten years? Twenty years? It's never too early to start shaping your goals and begin making them a reality. Just like we talked about in Chapter 2, it's important for you to dream BIG when you think about the future and what you want to accomplish. If your dreams don't scare you, they aren't big enough! So, keep dreaming and don't let anything hold you back. Write down the things that seem wild, unrealistic, or even impossible. If God's in it, he will make it happen.

I encourage you to think about dreams and goals in all the different areas of your life. You may have one central dream, but alongside that dream there are other important goals that contribute to your story. Where do you want to travel? What do you want to accomplish in your education? Are there any exciting adventures you want to have? Is there a hobby you've always wanted to try or a language you'd like to learn? These are all important goals to pursue too! You can even think about personal traits you'd like to develop, friendships you want to invest in, and goals for reading the Bible and serving in a church. Maintaining balance in life is such an important part of being happy and staying on track. So, think about all the areas of your life when you shape your goals and envision your dreams.

By now you know that I'm all about individuality and being the best you that you can be. Make sure you stay true to yourself as you dream and work toward your destiny. Don't be pressured into taking on other people's dreams for you if they don't fit with who you are. And don't be discouraged by negative feedback about your goals. When your goals are in harmony with who you are, they are the right goals for your life. That's why it's so important to take time for yourself to reflect, write, and talk to God in prayer. It will help you stay connected to the true you so you will be able to easily tell what fits with who you are and what doesn't. Never compromise or change who you are to achieve your dreams. An accomplished goal is only satisfying when you've done it with integrity.

As you mature and grow older, parts of you will change and develop, but the core of who you are is always there. Listen to that inner voice which comes from the Holy Spirit. Know your true self so well that you can notice very quickly when you're tempted or pressured to change who you are. There is nothing more rewarding than living your most authentic life!

And finally, here is your most important mission: use what you have learned in this book to go out in the world and make a difference! God has given you all your talents and gifts so you can impact people for good. Keep using your abilities to encourage, inspire, and build others up. If you face struggles along the way, don't let them beat you down because there is a greater purpose in everything you do. Keep shining your light, doing what you were made to do, and watch as your destiny has a ripple effect on everyone around you. Keep living a bold life and you will be blessed!

KEEP DREAMING

Remember those two dreams you made goals for in Chapter 2? Go back and read through them again. Spend some time thinking about both of them and writing down anything that comes to mind as you think.

1. Start with one of your dreams and think big—as big as you possibly can! Don't hold back anything because it scares you. Dream your wildest dreams!

2. Write down your big dream in bold letters on a piece of paper. Keep rewriting it until it feels just right and summarizes the desires of your heart. Copy the final sentence onto a piece of paper by itself. Post it somewhere that you can see it every day and read it out loud.

3. Start working toward your big dream by setting goals. First, set a goal for something you can achieve toward this dream in the next month.

It might be very simple, like doing research or taking lessons or classes to get started.

4. Next, set a goal for what you'd like to achieve in one year that will bring you closer to your dream. Maybe it's practicing a certain number of hours or performing in a small venue.

5. Now set a goal for what you'd like to achieve in three years that will bring you closer to your dream.

6. Repeat the previous steps for your second dream!

Continue to revisit your big dream and keep working toward setting bigger and bigger goals over the years. Keep praying as you work hard and don't be afraid to ask for help!

FAN Q & A

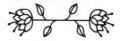

Q: How did you handle K.C. Undercover *ending?*

A: We knew going into the season that it was our last. So, it wasn't a shock when it was announced. The hard thing was after three years of being with the same people every day you become like a family. So that took a little getting used to with us not being together all the time.

• • • • • • •

Q: What is your dream college?

A: I have two dream colleges. One of them is the London Business School and the other is Harvard. One of my biggest dreams is to study abroad.

• • • • • • •

Q: If there is one thing you could change in the world, what would it be?

A: I would end all racism. I especially want our African-American men to be able to walk down the street or drive a car without fear of being killed.

Conclusion

Whether you're a friend, family member, supporter, or had never heard of me before, thank you for reading this book! I hope you've enjoyed some of the sneak peeks into my life as an actress. I hope some of my embarrassing moments made you laugh. Maybe you've had some of the same experiences I've had with family and friends, or maybe our lives are very different. I know God created me for a special purpose, and I know he created you for a special purpose too. No one else can be *you*. No one else can walk in your shoes and follow the path God has just for you.

I hope you have learned through this book that following God is not always easy. Waiting for God to show you what he wants you to do can take a while—even years. But whatever dream God has placed in your heart, it's a dream worth pursuing. Always stay true to who you are and surround yourself with people who will lift you up. Most of all, remember that God loves you more than anything, and he wants you to love him too.

And now, my friends, it's time for me to go, so that I can continue to grow!

Smooches, Trinitee

Journaling with Trinitee

I've shared a lot of my life with you, and thinking about it and writing it down has been good for me. Journaling is a great way to:

- Figure out how you feel about things
- Understand yourself better
- Relieve stress
- Work out your problems on paper before you have to in real life
- Put yourself in other people's shoes

On the next pages, I've come up with some journaling prompts for you, partly inspired by my fans' questions. I hope they help you as much as they've helped me. Happy journaling!

Smooches, Trinitee

Three goals I have set for myself (and why) are . . .

_____

_____

_____

_____

_____

_____

_____

_____

_____

_____

_____

_____

_____

_____

Write about a time in your life when you struggled with a choice and made the right one.

Make a list of 10 things you could do to show others God's love.

Describe an event that changed your life forever, or make up and describe an event that would change your life forever.

Write a list of at least 50 things that make you feel good.

What do you consider your greatest accomplishment to date and why?

Were you ever looking forward to something that turned out to be a disappointment? How did you deal with it?

Write about a time you were talked into something and later you regretted doing it.

Write about a time that someone close to you disappointed you. How did it make you feel? How do you think they felt?

If you could throw a party for all your friends, what would it be like? Where would you hold it? What would you do? Who would come?

Write about a rule at school or home that you don't like. How would you replace it?

_____

_____

_____

_____

_____

_____

_____

_____

_____

_____

_____

_____

_____

_____

_____

_____

_____

_____

_____

_____

_____

_____

_____

_____

_____

_____

If you could live anywhere in the world, where would it be?

What is your biggest fear?

_____

_____

_____

_____

_____

_____

_____

_____

_____

_____

_____

_____

_____

_____

_____

_____

_____

_____

_____

_____

_____

_____

_____

_____

_____

_____

What is one of the greatest challenges you've had to face, and how did you overcome it?

If you could change one thing about the world, what would it be? As a young person, how do you think you could make this happen?

_____

_____

_____

_____

_____

_____

_____

_____

_____

_____

_____

_____

_____

_____

_____

_____

_____

_____

_____

_____

_____

_____

Acknowledgments

Steve, Allison, & Nathan Kress, Courtney B. Vance, Crystal Bowman, Teri McKinley, my pastors Darryl Garrett and Michael J.T. Fisher, Tosha Moore, Stacey Donaldson, Torri Powell, Coach Shonneia Adams, Darrell Miller, Rick Smith, Tiffanie Diamond, Rhonda Garrett, Tongie Scott, my wonderful grandparents, wise great-aunts/uncle, Felicia Brookins, Eric Everett, Rob Lotterstein, Al & Hattie Hollingsworth, and every member of my team.

Special thanks to someone I admire in so many ways, Mrs. Angela Bassett. You are a true inspiration and example of strength, beauty, and grace. Thank you for always showing love to my family.

Thanks to my mentor Lisa Nichols for helping me to break down barriers so that I am able to dip. (smile)

In loving memory of my auntie Jerri Thomas, my acting coach Cheryl Faye, and our wonderful family friend Wynter Evans Pitts. I thank God for you being vessels used by God to pour into me and guide me along the way. Thanks for all of the fun and laughs. Ms. Wynter, thanks for that infamous elevator ride. :o) My life was made better because of all of you.

Thanks to all of my friends and family that have been traveling with me on my great adventure! Let's see where we are off to next!

STAY CONNECTED WITH ME!

 @the_trinitee

 @the_trinitee

 Trinitee Stokes

 @the_trinitee

 Trinitee Stokes

 www.thetrinitee.com